'This treasure trove of ideas is ...rth in organisational coaching a ...by powerful and diverse case stu...., uus uook forms a courageous attempt at pinpointing the kinds of leaders and leadership we need for the future. *Creating a Coaching Culture* helps those future-oriented leaders to think about how executive coaching may help bring out the organisational changes that we need to keep adapting to ever more demanding challenges'.
– **Erik de Haan**, *Director of Ashridge Centre for Coaching and Professor of Organisational Development, VU University*

'*Creating a Coaching Culture for Managers in Your Organisation* is a very welcome and timely addition to the literature on the theme of coaching. In a practical, non-prescriptive manner the authors provide a wealth of experience and guidance to help those working on this challenge. With several of the examples taken from the authors' work in the world of higher education the book will find a ready audience in this sector, from senior academic leaders to HR professionals and leadership development specialists. Practising what they preach there is no 10 point, silver bullet, plan – what you do get , however, are some incisive questions to help you explore and develop your own distinctive culture of coaching. Highly recommended'.
– **Dr Tom Kennie**, *Director of Ranmore Consulting and Programme Director of the Leadership Foundation for Higher Education Top Management Programme (TMP)*

'This innovative and highly practical book is essential reading for busy managers. It focuses on the critical task of bringing about real and lasting culture change, improved performance and whole organisation transformation through coaching. I have been looking for such a clear and comprehensive book to assist me as a CEO for a long time – this book is a must for staying ahead of the coaching curve'.
– **Lynne Sedgmore CBE**, *Chief Executive of 157 Group*

'This book offers a well-articulated set of perspectives on the importance of coaching and the impact it can make on behaviours and cultures in organisations. It will give courage to those who are determined to enable the best performance from colleagues, and practical new perspectives from a wide range of different sectors. This is a gift for the committed "learning leader"'.
– **Dr Paul Gentle**, *Director of Programmes, Leadership Foundation for Higher Education UK*

145690

'This book provides a comprehensive overview of coaching, how it can be implemented and the potential benefits it offers an organisation. It provides an opportunity for leaders to reflect on what they are doing in their own organisation and the importance of establishing a culture that supports staff engagement and empowerment'.
– **Clory Carrello,** *Chief Executive Officer, Cockburn GP Super Clinic, Perth, Australia*

'Great to see a book in the coaching field that goes beyond the individual and helps organisations develop the kind of culture that makes life liveable for managers and employees alike. This is a book that should be read by all interested in creating a coaching type culture for managers in all sorts of organisations – a must buy book'.
– **Professor Cary L. Cooper, CBE,** *Distinguished Professor of Organizational Psychology and Health at Lancaster University Management School, Chair of the Academy of Social Sciences, President of the British Association of Counselling and Psychotherapy and President of RELATE*

'This book emphasizes the importance of coaching development and recognizes it is about establishing a Culture through new skills and knowledge for effective change and leadership direction. A highly practical guide for developing coaches'.
– **Professor Marion Jones,** *Dean, University Postgraduate Studies and Academic Leader, Manukau Campus, Manutaki o Ngā Akoranga Pia o Te Wānanga, New Zealand*

'*Creating a Coaching Culture* provides a detailed rationale for building and maintaining a foundation of coaching in organisations – it is a really useful handbook covering the why, what and how. The real-world case studies, practical guidance and realistic strategies illustrate simple ways to successfully implement coaching to effect change across the complex layers of an organisation's operations'.
– **Anna Reader,** *National Coordinator, Women's Executive Development (WEXDEV), Australian Technology Network of Universities (ATN)*

'If you are looking for a practical, no-nonsense guide to helping those with a stake in the firm and questions about the value of a coaching culture, then this is the book for you.'
– **David Megginson,** *Emeritus Professor of Human Resource Development, Sheffield Business School,* from the Foreword

Creating a Coaching Culture for Managers in Your Organisation

Creating a Coaching Culture for Managers in Your Organisation is for managers, leaders and coaches interested in extending the practice of coaching to achieve broader organisational outcomes. The book offers a practical approach on how to use coaching strategically to create a culture that supports change, builds leadership capacity and achieves a high degree of alignment between the goals and aspirations of organisations and their staff.

The authors provide rich case study examples of how coaching has been used in a range of organisations to build leadership capacity and learning, and support new ways of working. Taken together, the chapters provide insight into how organisations can develop a culture that promotes engagement, open and dialogic communication, clarity of expectations and high performance.

This valuable text is a timely contribution to current thinking on leadership, management and organisation development. It will be of interest to managers, leaders, HR professionals and coaching professionals, as well as students interested in coaching techniques, counsellors and psychotherapists.

Dawn Forman has worked as an independent executive coach and consultant for five years and is an adjunct professor at Curtin University and Auckland University of Technology, and a visiting professor at Auckland University of Technology.

Mary Joyce is an executive coach, leadership consultant and Director of Leading Minds Consulting. She teaches the psychodynamics of groups and organisational behaviour, and is visiting tutor at Salomons, Canterbury Christ Church University.

Gladeana McMahon is one of the leading coaches in the UK. She is a co-editor of the *Essential Coaching Skills and Knowledge* series.

Essential Coaching Skills and Knowledge
Series Editors: Gladeana McMahon,
Stephen Palmer and Averil Leimon

The **Essential Coaching Skills and Knowledge** series provides an accessible and lively introduction to key areas in the developing field of coaching. Each title in the series is written by leading coaches with extensive experience and has a strong practical emphasis, including illustrative vignettes, summary boxes, exercises and activities. Assuming no prior knowledge, these books will appeal to professionals in business, management, human resources, psychology, counselling and psychotherapy, as well as students and tutors of coaching and coaching psychology.

www.routledgementalhealth.com/essential-coaching-skills

Titles in the series:

Essential Business Coaching
Averil Leimon, François Moscovici and Gladeana McMahon

**Achieving Excellence in Your Coaching Practice:
How to Run a Highly Successful Coaching Business**
Gladeana McMahon, Stephen Palmer and Christine Wilding

**A Guide to Coaching and Mental Health: The Recognition
and Management of Psychological Issues**
Andrew Buckley and Carole Buckley

Essential Life Coaching Skills
Angela Dunbar

101 Coaching Strategies
Edited by Gladeana McMahon and Anne Archer

Group and Team Coaching
Christine Thornton

Coaching Women to Lead
Averil Leimon, François Moscovici and Helen Goodier

**Developmental Coaching: Life Transitions and
Generational Perspectives**
Edited by Stephen Palmer and Sheila Panchal

**Cognitive Behavioural Coaching in Practice:
An Evidence Based Approach**
Edited by Michael Neenan and Stephen Palmer

Brief Coaching: A Solution Focused Approach
Chris Iveson, Evan George and Harvey Ratner

Interactional Coaching
Michael Harvey

Solution Focused Coaching in Practice
Bill O'Connell, Stephen Palmer and Helen Williams

Coaching with Meaning and Spirituality
Peter Hyson

Creating a Coaching Culture for Managers in Your Organisation

Edited by Dawn Forman, Mary Joyce and Gladeana McMahon

LONDON AND NEW YORK

First published 2013
by Routledge
27 Church Road, Hove, East Sussex BN3 2FA

Simultaneously published in the USA and Canada
by Routledge
711 Third Avenue, New York, NY 10017

Routledge is an imprint of the Taylor & Francis Group, an informa business

British Library Cataloguing in Publication Data
A catalogue record for this book is available from the British Library

Library of Congress Cataloging in Publication Data
Creating a coaching culture for managers in your organisation /
edited by Dawn Forman, Mary Joyce, and Gladeana McMahon.
       p. cm. — (Essential coaching skills and knowledge)
    Includes bibliographical references and index.
  1. Employees—Coaching of. 2. Corporate culture.
  3. Organizational behavior. 4. Management. I. Forman, Dawn,
  1957– II. Joyce, Mary, 1959– III. McMahon, Gladeana.
  HF5549.5.C53C74 2013
  658.4′07124—dc23   2012036790

ISBN: 978–0–415–69021–8 (hbk)
ISBN: 978–0–415–69022–5 (pbk)
ISBN: 978–0–203–42251–9 (ebk)

Typeset in New Century Schoolbook
by Swales & Willis Ltd, Exeter, Devon

MIX
Paper from
responsible sources
FSC
www.fsc.org   FSC® C013056

Printed and bound in Great Britain by
TJ International Ltd, Padstow, Cornwall

Contents

Illustrations

About the contributors

Deborah Fleming is an entrepreneur and the founder of Chameleon Works, a consultancy specialising in supporting organisations, teams and individuals during transformation and change. She created the 'Personality of Wine', a leadership event combining Myers-Briggs Type Indicator and wine tasting, following her experience as lead trainer with OPP. Her international consultancy experience has taken her to the USA and Europe, working for both private and public organisations. She holds an Advanced Diploma in Executive Coaching, and coaches in a variety of contexts and development programmes, recently supporting IBM, SAB Miller and an Oxfordshire primary school to incorporate coaching into their cultures. She has an MSc in Organisational Development and Change, and has presented at a number of conferences on change management.

Dawn Foreman has recently returned to the UK from Australia where she was working as Clinical Director and Professor at Curtin University in Perth for 15 months. Dawn resumes her international consultancy from her base in Sheffield, England and remains a Key Associate of the Leadership Foundation for Higher Education (UK), a Senior Associate of Ranmore Consulting (UK) and Feldman and Associates (Aus). In her consultancy Dawn specialises in executive coaching, leadership development, scenario planning and team development at board and senior leadership levels.

In addition to her consultancy, Dawn has experience of using her coaching skills in her executive leadership roles which have been both in universities and in the health care services. Dawn was a Dean of Faculty for 13 years and has served on a number of boards, provided governor development and coaching provision and managed departments of up to 550 staff.

Dawn is currently recognised at professorial levels in three universities internationally. This is her fifth book, and she has published a number of chapters and over 40 articles in peer-reviewed journals. Dawn has a number of academic qualifications including a PhD, MBA and both a Post Graduate Diploma and Accreditation in Executive Coaching.

Mary Joyce trained in process consultation, organisational behaviour and group dynamics at the Tavistock & Portman NHS Foundation Trust, and as an executive coach at Ashridge Business School. She also has training in psychotherapy and counselling. Mary has supported clients at all stages of the change process and teaches on the psychodynamics of change, groups and organisations. She has held a number of leadership roles at the Tavistock and Portman NHS Foundation Trust, Thames Valley University, and the Sector Skills Council for Lifelong Learning. The national leadership programme she designed and led for principals/chief executive officers in the further education sector embedded a culture of coaching during a vital phase of change. As Director of Leading Minds Consulting, her reputation for working 'beneath the surface' has developed through a variety of leadership and consultancy experiences in the private and public sectors. Mary is a member of the European Mentoring and Coaching Council, and is a Fellow of the Chartered Management Institute and the Royal Society of Arts.

Gladeana McMahon holds a range of qualifications as a therapist and coach and was instrumental in helping found the Association for Coaching, for which she holds the positions of Life Fellow and Chair. She is also a Fellow of the British Association for Counselling and Psychotherapy, the Institute of Management Studies and the Royal Society of Arts. An innovator, Gladeana is one of the UK founders of Cognitive Behavioural Coaching and is an internationally published author of over 18 books of a popular and academic nature on coaching and counselling.

Graham Megson is Dean of School at the University of Westminster, and a certified trainer of neuro-linguistic programming (NLP). He has extensive experience of leading change programmes within universities and significant management experience at all levels of academia, from research-intensive to teaching-led universities. He has an MBA, and is a freelance consultant in personal and team development with Maple Tree House. Graham originally trained as a computer scientist, and was Reader in Parallel Computing at Newcastle University, Research Fellow at Oxford University and Professor of Computer Science at Reading University. He has published widely and is a Fellow of the British Computer Society, a Chartered Engineer and a Chartered IT Professional. He sits on a number of editorial boards for scientific journals, as well as reviewing papers for the NLP Research Conference.

Janice Steed, of Steed Consulting Ltd, has over 30 years' experience as a clinician and senior leader of high-performing teams. She now works as an organisation consultant and executive coach, supporting leadership development, organisation and culture change programmes within and outside the public sector. Her work is strongly informed by her experience as a midwife, and she has a facilitative approach to 'working with' and not 'doing to' clients to help them realise their potential. She is experienced in clinical leadership and commissioning development, supporting effective team development as well as individual coaching. Janice is a trained nurse and midwife, with an Advanced Diploma in Midwifery and an MSc in Organisational Consulting from Ashridge Business School, where she also trained as an executive coach.

Gwen Wileman is a highly experienced HR Director, facilitator and executive coach. She has held the role of HR Director in three sectors; she has been an HR management academic at Leicester Business School and consultant in leadership, management development and business at the UK Post Office National Leadership College. Her current clients include Aston University, University of Wolverhampton, CHEAD (Council for Higher Education in Art and Design) and universities HR. Gwen is a Fellow of the Chartered Institute of Personnel and Development and an accredited executive coach. She was a member of the Universities Human Resources (UHR) national executive, and national lead for HR continuing professional development. Gwen has been awarded a Leadership Fellowship from the Leadership Foundation for Higher Education, and is an author and a regular conference contributor.

Foreword

*David Megginson, Emeritus Professor
of Human Resource Development,
Sheffield Business School*

I offer a warm welcome to this book on creating a coaching culture for managers. Since David Clutterbuck and I wrote our book on the subject there has been slow progress in developing the theme of creating a coaching culture. I see this as being caused at least in part by coaches' privileging the individual at the expense of the collective. This book fills the gap in terms of focusing on the manager's experience of having a responsibility for contributing to a coaching culture. This focus – on the people responsible for the vast majority of the coaching that goes on – is healthy and useful.

The tone of this book is pragmatic and down to earth. You will not be faced with daunting theory or rigid prescriptions. Rather, readers will find clear and helpful guidance on steps that need to be taken. There is a chapter on using external coaches but it is where it belongs – at the end of the book!

If you are asking questions about coaching culture like 'What's in it for me?' or 'What are the pitfalls?' or 'How do I develop a supportive culture in my part of the organisation?' then this is the book for you. I like the way the authors do not dodge the challenges and the objections that will be put and take these on in a robust manner.

I also welcome the recognition of the part of action learning in building a coaching culture. My experience indicates that this intervention seals in the gains that can be initiated by skills training, but somehow needs consolidation.

The authors have been careful to offer a range of approaches and frameworks in a non-doctrinaire way. These are accessible to someone new to coaching and will reinforce learning and practice helpfully.

So, if you are looking for a practical, no-nonsense guide to helping those with a stake in the organisation and questions about the value of a coaching culture, then this is the book for you.

David Megginson
Sheffield, August 2012

Preface

The last 20 years have seen a rapid increase in the use of coaching in organisations, and a corresponding growth in the number of books available on the subject. Some of these books are directed at managers and tend to have a specific focus on 'performance coaching', in other words, using coaching to enhance the performance of individuals to achieve specific goals. In writing this book we wanted to shift the focus to a more strategic application of coaching in organisations, as a response to the marked changes that are taking place in the world, in our organisations and in our work.

This book is for managers, leaders and coaches in the public and private sectors, and offers a practical approach to extending the benefits of coaching to support wider organisational change and practice, and to create a coaching culture. A recent study conducted by the Institute of Leadership and Management (*Creating a Coaching Culture*, 2010) showed that although 53 per cent of the organisations in its survey used coaching for general personal development, only 12 per cent used it to support organisational objectives and even fewer (4 per cent) used it to support organisational transformation. There is clearly an even greater benefit to be realised in introducing the skills associated with coaching more widely into the organisations: 'Organisations wishing to maximise the benefits of coaching should focus on increasing its scope and availability to create a coaching culture that permeates throughout their workforce.'

The theme of leadership and a changed (and changing) world runs throughout the book, and is developed in some depth in the first chapter. This also contextualises the practice of coaching, as we see it, for the other chapters in the book. The acute socio-political, economic and technological scale of change taking place worldwide has an impact on how we do business and how we lead in our organisations. The pressures on managers and leaders to deal with mergers, restructuring, constant change, uncertainty and paradox mean that the old 'command and control' and 'pace setting' (as described by Daniel Goleman in *The New Leaders*, 2002) ways of leading, managing and relating in the workplace will not achieve the level of transformational change and adaptability that is required to survive and thrive in more unpredictable and uncertain times.

Several chapters in the book show how coaching can alter the quality of relationships in an organisation, in turn changing its culture. They demonstrate the potential that is available in organisations by tapping into the seam of creativity that lies in their people. One of the characteristics of our changing world is the changing nature of the problems we face. Complex and intractable problems are more likely to find sustainable solutions when people work together and collaborate to co-create the future. The nature of these problems makes them too complex for one person alone to manage and deal with; the same can be said of organisational change.

The book embraces the philosophy and theory of building leadership capability at every level of the organisation. This can be achieved by helping each and every individual or team to see and contribute the best they have to offer, through the development of greater emotional intelligence. The book provides rich case study examples of how coaching has been used by a range of organisations to build capacity for leadership and learning, and to support new ways of working. We also show how an organisation can introduce coaching with good intentions but manage to undermine the initiative and limit its effectiveness through the way it operates its organisational processes. Readers will see that the strategic use of coaching can lead to a greater alignment between the aims and ambitions of staff and those of the organisation, resulting in greater productivity and job satisfaction.

In this book we also tackle more practical issues, such as why some managers may be reluctant to use coaching as part of their practice, the pros and cons of coaching, some simple guidance on how to get started, and an exploration of some of the circumstances when it is advisable to refer a coachee to another professional, and when to use an external coach. Research now shows that empowering staff through coaching can lead to more successful organisations. We include a chapter with advice on how to measure the success of coaching when it has been introduced into the organisation.

In this book we embrace leadership theories which look at employee engagement as a means to both understanding employees within organisations and ensuring that attention is paid to the ways in which an alignment is achieved and created between the values, culture, philosophy, mission, vision, targets and overall aspirations of the organisation and employees.

Taken together, the chapters we have assembled here argue that creating a coaching culture within an organisation will develop a culture of motivation and engagement. A culture where each member of staff experiences communication as positive, open, dialogic and non-judgemental, and where clarity of aspirations and expectations, both of the individual and the organisation, can be achieved.

In coming together to write this book we are aware of being a 'broad church' of contributors, representing an eclectic approach to how we think about and practise coaching. We found a great deal of synergy and pleasure in our collaboration, and hope that you enjoy the variety of voices in the book and that we have provided you with some 'food for thought'.

Dawn Forman
Mary Joyce
Gladeana McMahon
Editors, 2012

1

The changing world
in which we live

Dawn Forman

In this fast-paced, complex and ever competitive world people need different and more individualised ways of supporting their needs and helping organisations change and adapt to the increasing pressures and constraints. As such, many organisations are incorporating coaching as a key to helping their employees to both grow and develop new ways of working and to help them, as individuals and collectively in organisations as a whole, to cope with the considerable changes which are impacting upon them. In order to better understand why this may be the case we need to understand the factors affecting organisations and the changes in leadership which are being demanded.

Environmental influences

When organisations embark on strategic planning to position themselves for the future they often undertake an environmental analysis, which takes into account a whole variety of factors that could impact on the organisation to a greater or lesser extent. This is often known as a PEST analysis, as Political, Economic, Social and Technological influences are reviewed. Johnson, Scholes and Whittington (2006) take this a stage further by listing a range of wider environmental considerations, as shown in the adapted diagram (Figure 1.1).

Many organisations undertaking this review in current times indicate that prospects look pretty bleak. Indeed, the present climate has been described as a 'perfect storm' or

Figure 1.1 Examples of environmental influences (adapted from Johnson, Scholes and Whittington, 2006)

considerable 'climate change', as there are a number of critical factors occurring at the same time.

With a perfect storm, the view would be that this difficult time will soon pass and we will then be able to return to our 'normal' way of working. This supposes that there is a 'normal way of working'; however, even in less extreme times different individuals and external factors must always be considered and adapted to. The impact of the changes we are currently facing, however, is more far-reaching and we may never be able to return to what we used to describe as 'normal'. Hence the term which will be used here is 'significant climate change' rather than 'a perfect storm'.

If we undertake what is traditionally known as a PEST or environmental analysis there are a number of challenging components that we can see need to be taken into account to a greater or lesser extent, depending on the particular context of the organisation. These are summarised in Figure 1.2.

The number of clouds indicates the factors which need to be taken into account and therefore the considerable change environment in which all organisations within the UK are now working.

This can be seen as a very bleak prospect for organisations, and particularly the leaders of organisations, as they cope with a considerable downturn in the economy, and indeed in their business, with little prospect of the growth

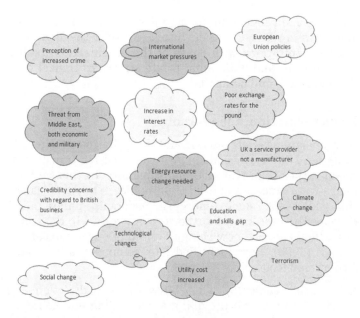

Figure 1.2 **Perfect storm or climate change**

that they may have been used to over the past decade. Many leaders are not equipped with the skills to cope with this change in direction and are either having to re-skill or rethink their futures.

This in itself has caused an increase in the number of leaders who are now seeking to redevelop themselves through leadership programmes or, working with a coach to help them, through structured space and time to cope with and adapt to the change. Executive coaching has, therefore, seen an increase within this economic climate, either in helping leaders with the change they are personally undergoing, for instance if they are leaving their current post to retire or to take on a different post in a different organisation, or in helping leaders develop opportunities for themselves and their organisation in this climate of change.

In addition to looking at the focus for leaders, leaders in turn need to consider how the managers within their organisations are also coping with this considerable change. Again, coaching can provide an opportunity for those leaders and managers to reconsider their future, consider the alignment of their aspirations with those of the organisation, realise opportunities and build appropriate strategies to deal with the new needs and demands.

Transformational leadership

If organisations are to survive and thrive in this climate new skills need to be embedded, with the need for transformational rather than transactional capability. In this we have seen a resurgence of some old philosophies in terms of leadership skills and some emerging leadership philosophies. Perhaps the best-known authority with regard to the transformational change now being required of our organisations is Bass (1999). Bass identified four components for transformational leadership:

- *Idealised leadership* The ability to set a direction and articulate a vision providing a compelling and coherent view of the future.
- *Inspirational motivation* Providing a role model inspiring respect, trust, loyalty and confidence and igniting passion, pace and drive.
- *Intellectual stimulation* Providing stretching aspirations and targets for staff, encouraging them to think through problems and find solutions and alternative ways of working.
- *Individualised consideration* Treating everyone with respect and recognising differences in abilities, motivations and aspirations.

If we think of great leaders, those that have achieved transformational change, a name which is often brought to mind is Nelson Mandela.

Nelson Mandela is best known for his fight against apartheid, but when he emerged from prison and became president of South Africa he faced a different challenge in terms of his leadership skills. He needed to unite the country and ensure black and white worked together to make the country economically viable as a nation.

One tactic he used in creating a vision and inspiring motivation was to provide an achievable but stretching objective with a shared goal (Case Study 1.1; Carlin, 2007). Recognising how individual aspirations could be harnessed in order to achieve, he used a concept that the whole country would own. This was the challenge he gave to host the Rugby World Cup, believing in what it would bring in practice and also what it would symbolise as a way of coming together across the country and the black and white divide.

Case Study 1.1   How Nelson Mandela won the Rugby World Cup

It was a Herculean political challenge but in the Rugby World Cup, to be played in South Africa a year after he came to power, Mandela saw an opportunity not to be missed.

The African National Congress had spent years using rugby as a stick with which to beat white people (talk to any prominent Afrikaner from those days and they will tell you how much the international rugby boycott hurt). Mandela said: 'Why not use it now as a carrot? Why not use the Springbok team to unite the most divided nation on earth around a common goal?'

So, barely a month after he had taken office, he invited François Pienaar, the Springbok captain, for tea at his office in Pretoria. He wooed him instantly: 'I felt like a wide-eyed kid listening to an old man telling stories', Pienaar told me, and without the big blond son of apartheid quite knowing it yet, Mandela recruited him to the new South Africa cause.

Mandela's challenges not only lay on the white side of the apartheid fence. He had to do some tough political persuasion among his own black supporters too. They had been brought up to detest rugby. Next to the old anthem and the old flag, there existed no more repellent symbol of apartheid than the green Springbok shirt. That was why the blacks-only pens at rugby stadiums were always full on international match days, cheering the Springboks' opponents.

But Mandela set himself the mission of converting black South Africans to the perplexing notion that the 'Boks belonged to all of us now', as he put it to me. And this even though he knew that the team for the 1995 World Cup would be all white, with the possible exception of a 'coloured' wing called Chester Williams.

'They booed me!', Mandela recalled, chuckling only long after the event. 'My own people, they booed me when I stood before them, urging them to support the Springboks!' But eventually, Mandela being a natural-born persuader and black South Africans an amazingly forgiving lot, he achieved his goal. Come the morning of the final, on 24 June 1995, black South Africans were as excited as their white compatriots, and as desperate to see the *Amabokoboko* (as the Sowetan newspaper dubbed the national team) win.

Pienaar and company deserved much of the credit for this. The clever, politically sharp CEO of the South African Rugby Union, Edward Griffiths, had come up with a slogan that was brilliant in its simplicity: 'One team, one country'.

Morné du Plessis, a former Springbok captain and now team manager, had worked hard to make the players see that they had a role to play in helping Mandela unite the country. It was du Plessis who arranged for the players to learn the old song of black resistance, now the new national anthem, *Nkosi Sikelel' iAfrika* ('God Bless Africa'). At a choir session in Cape Town, the Springbok players belted out the black song with feeling, the vast second-row Boer Kobus Wiese leading the choral charge.

As the World Cup unfolded, following a great inaugural victory by South Africa over Australia, the players, as well as the white fans, were struck by the growing enthusiasm of the hitherto rugby-illiterate black population. The sight of those vast Boers singing their song at the start of each game and then winning it was a combination increasingly difficult for black South Africans to resist. This in turn nourished the Afrikaners' budding sense of new South African fellow feeling.

Mandela's *coup de grâce*, which ensured the final submission of white South Africa to his charms, came minutes before the final itself, when the old terrorist-in-chief went on to the pitch to shake hands with the players, dressed in the colours of the ancient enemy – the green Springbok shirt. For a moment, Ellis Park Stadium, 95 per cent white on the day, stood in dumb, disbelieving silence. Then someone took up a cry that others followed, ending in a thundering roar: 'Nel-son! Nel-son! Nel-son!'

And that was almost it. White South Africa had crowned Mandela king with the fervour black South Africa had done five years earlier at a stadium in Soweto, in the week after his release. But there was still the matter of a game to be played against a formidable New Zealand team. And, in the view of every sane rugby pundit alive, the Springboks did not stand a chance.

They were wrong. With Mandela playing as an invisible 16th man, Joel Stransky, the one Jewish player in the Springbok team, kicked the winning drop goal in extra time. Mandela emerged again, still in his green jersey, and, to even louder cries of 'Nel-son! Nel-son!', walked on to the pitch to shake the hand of François Pienaar.

As he prepared to hand over the cup to his captain, he said: 'François, thank you for what you have done for our country.' Pienaar, with extraordinary presence of mind, replied: 'No, Mr President. Thank you for what you have done.'

(Carlin, 2007; reproduced with permission)

This was a transformation change of seismic proportion.

Mandela and Pienaar transformed the aspirations of the rugby players; they both understood how important it was for the country and indeed for every South African to have a vision, stretching targets and stimulating and inspirational individualised motivators. Their relationship seems to have been one of mutual or peer coaching, with Pienaar translating his leadership coaching into the coaching he undertook with the team.

When we speak of leading a sports team we will in the next breath automatically speak of coaching the team to success. Pienaar was the leader of the team – the captain, the coach – and he used coaching techniques to inspire, motivate and train the Springboks.

In turn Mandela coached Pienaar, raising both his aspirations and his self-belief. Collectively, they gained a following which eventually owned the goals they were trying to achieve.

Can this transformational leadership approach be used in everyday leadership?

Earlier we indicated the enormous challenge we are facing in our 'significant climate change' and perhaps unsurprisingly we are therefore finding new theories of leadership emerging. This new leadership concentrates on the employees in the organisation to enhance employee engagement.

What is employee engagement and how does it link with transformational leadership?

> *Engagement is defined as a state of mind, an attitude which manifests through the behaviours and characteristics of the employee.*
>
> (Khan, 1990)

Figure 1.3 shows how employee engagement is formed from component parts; the traits of transformational leadership can be identified in the terms used. Fundamentally, coaching is indicated as a component.

Emotional intelligence

From the work of Goleman (1998) we are aware of how great a contribution emotional intelligence makes to good leadership. By emotional intelligence we mean that the leader is aware of their own feelings and how expressions and behaviours impact on others. They are also able to detect and understand the emotions of those who work close to them and indeed the emotions of clients or customers. Working with these emotions in a truly authentic and caring way, Goleman indicates, is a much more powerful tool than other leadership qualities. Establishing a coaching culture feeds emotional intelligence. The leader or manager, as the coach, needs to understand the emotions, feelings and atmosphere they are creating when in discussion with the coachee. Equally, they

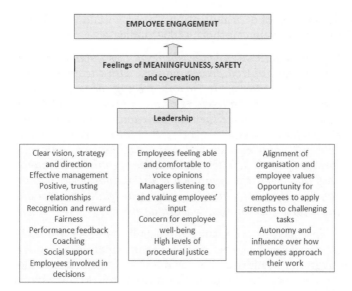

Figure 1.3 **The formation of employee engagement (Hockey and Ley, 2010)**

need to be very sensitive to not only what is said by the coachee but also the body language and feelings the coachee is expressing. While the coaching exercise is in a confidential environment, the understanding the manager will gain of the coachee and the coachee's motivations and aspirations can be very powerful in helping to ensure that the coachee's aspirations are aligned with those of the organisation.

Authentic leadership

In line with emotional intelligence, authentic leaders are in tune with their own emotions, aspirations and values, and those of their staff and customers. Their values are articulated openly and their actions match those articulated values through deep understanding of their own needs and requirements and those of others. They are able to unleash individual potential, create confidence and hope, raise optimism, strengthen resilience and, by empowering staff, enable the organisation to grow and develop. As Gardner and Schermerhorn (2004) indicate:

> *True authenticity in leadership requires the maturity to give up self-centred preoccupations with the efforts and failures of others. It means freeing oneself of the presumption that a leader's primary task is somehow to motivate others as if they were incapable of doing it for themselves. It means accepting that the leader's primary role is to value and support human talent in a high performance context. The practicalities of authentic leadership and a positive approach to individual performance can be truly exhilarating for you as the leader, and for all those fortunate enough to work with you.*

In coaching, the same philosophy is used. We believe that everyone has the answers, the capabilities and the motivations to address their own issues. Coaching provides a means of opening the door to unleash that knowledge and capability.

Employee engagement

The dialogue taking place with regard to employee engagement builds on transformational leadership, emotional intelligence and authentic leadership. It encompasses the notion that coaching can be a format to unleash the expertise of individuals but adds a further dimension, that of storytelling. Hockey and Ley (2010) outline how transformational leadership and authentic leadership, coupled with storytelling, help to empower and engage employees. Storytelling added to an already vibrant mixture of leadership skills can help to engage employees because it gives them a clearer understanding of the concept which the leader is trying to articulate. If a story can be told around the concept the storytelling is, in essence, facilitating the communication.

Weiss (1999) outlined storytelling in terms of effective narrative – a narrative which facilitates the articulation of the common values of employees and puts the challenges being faced into perspective. Denning (2006) builds upon this by indicating that narratives can spark action to get buy-in and allow new methods and approaches to be implemented. Stories are usually brief stories, positive in tone, and can communicate complex ideas when applied to a situation. These stories, which have been termed 'spring board' stories by Denning, allow listeners to build new narratives and set their own context where they develop action plans for implementing change. The story of Nelson Mandela's approach with the Springboks is one such story. It encapsulates how, if correctly motivated with key underpinning values, the seemingly impossible can be achieved by a great leader.

Again, stories can be told within a coaching context. Indeed, the coachee can be encouraged to tell his or her own stories and through this a greater understanding can be gained, both for the coachee and for the person coaching the individual. All the factors that have just been described are articulated in Figure 1.4; the outer ring of coaching and reflection is what we are trying to encourage through this book and indeed in developing a coaching culture within an organisation.

Good communication is also important for engaging with staff. The Cabinet Office (2009) carried out a review of the evidence base for employee engagement during 2007 as part of its work on improving engagement with civil servants

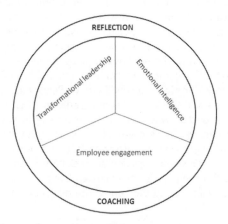

Figure 1.4 **Factors for employee engagement**

across all government departments. It showed that engaged staff are 43 per cent more productive, perform up to 20 per cent more effectively and take an average of 3.5 fewer sick days a year than disengaged staff.

Case Study 1.2 shows how a small Australian organisation uses coaching techniques along with emotional intelligence and employee engagement to create a transformational change, overcome the difficulties of the international economic climate and create a loyal customer base.

Case Study 1.2   Transformational change: Jo Jacaranda Garden Centre*, Perth, Australia

*Name changed at the request of the organisation.

The downturn in the economy has not affected Australia to the same extent as other countries, and Perth is still projecting growth in population, house prices and industry development, particularly through the mining industry.

Some organisations suffer from the isolated nature of Perth. International partnerships are difficult to maintain as the city is so distant from other countries and even from Eastern Australia. The owner, Susie, has tried to source supplies from overseas and build international partnerships but has had difficulties in getting the services she needs. She wonders about communication issues and the lack of face-to-face contact opportunity. The overseas suppliers must be doing well in their own countries, outside the tough trading conditions here in Perth, and not need the new business opportunities.

Although the summer sun can be harsh and bush fires are a constant consideration, the residents of Perth take a pride in their gardens and there has been a tradition of ensuring that even the restricted water is put to good use in keeping the gardens beautiful. The growth of large do-it-yourself organisations selling garden furniture and plants has, however, meant that some of the smaller garden centres have been challenged to survive. But the Jo Jacaranda Garden Centre is an exception and as you walk around the centre the difference here is very striking:

Staff: Hi, are you looking for anything in particular?
Customer: No just wandering round to get ideas.
Staff: That's fine. Let me know if I can help as we are happy to advise.
Customer: Well, we have just moved in to Applecross and have an established garden but want to add some colour to it and are worried about the sandy soil.
Staff: Yes, sand is a problem and perhaps helping the soil is a good place to start. Can I show you something?

The conversation moves on with a demonstration of a clear, chemical understanding of the soil conditions, examples of the types of plants which would work, an outline of what will look good with what and some ideas for saving money by taking cuttings rather than buying all the plants needed. A few things are purchased but the customer leaves feeling he/she has learnt a lot and almost made a friend as the discussion has progressed to the amount of time the customer has to spend in the garden and to family life and enjoying the outdoor environment.

As the customer leaves, the shop assistant who helps carry the goods to the car ensures the customer has the details of the shop, the website and email details and encourages the customer to email with any queries or challenges they are facing. An ongoing customer relationship is therefore established.

So why is the customer service arranged in this way? Susie Lawson the owner explains that she selects each member of her staff very carefully. Each staff member *must* be passionate, not only about gardening but about people as well. She feels the empathy and relationship the staff have with the customer is more important than making a sale! If a relationship is established the customer is more likely to return and make a commitment to the company because they feel as if they are friends of the organisation. Susie encourages her staff to tap into their emotional intelligence and to understand what the customer actually wants. Susie ensures staff keep up to speed with new technologies and fashions in gardens, and that they tour Perth to understand the climate and conditions customers may be facing and gather ideas on their travels.

'Demonstrating they know about the area where the customer lives again gives the customer confidence', Susie says, and finally and perhaps most importantly Susie coaches her staff to understand their own feelings about gardening – what motivates them, what a difference the garden looking good makes to them and their families – and encourages her staff to coach the customers into understanding their own feelings and to problem-solve for themselves. With such a philosophy the Jo Jacaranda Garden Centre has not only grown on its initial site but has now established five other sites in Perth, which all work on the same philosophy of coaching combined with passion.

Conclusion

With the impact of the considerable changes which all organisations are facing, new ways of leading and managing staff are being generated. We are learning from past leadership models and incorporating transformational change, emotional intelligence, storytelling and employee engagement into our thinking. Key to creating leadership development capacity in our organisations will be ensuring our leaders reflect on and learn from their experiences and encourage employees to think through the factors affecting their area of the organisation for themselves. Coaching leaders is therefore a key aspect of creating a learning organisation for the future changes which we are facing.

References

Bass, B. M. (1999) Two decades of research and development in transformational leadership. *European Journal of Work and Organizational Psychology*, 8(8), 9–32.

Cabinet Office (2009) *Leadership*. London: Cabinet Office.

Carlin, J. (2007) How Nelson Mandela won the Rugby World Cup. *The Telegraph,* 19 October.

Denning, S. (2006) Effective story telling: Strategic business narrative techniques. *Strategy and Leadership*, 34(1), 42–48.

Gardner, W. L. and Schermerhorn, J. R. (2004) Unleashing individual potential: Performance gains through positive organisational behavior and authentic leadership. *Organizational Dynamics*, 33(3), 270–281.

Goleman, D. (1998) What makes a leader? *Harvard Business Review*, November–December, 93–102.

Hockey, J. and Ley, I. (2010) *Leading for Engagement: How Senior Leaders Engage Their People: A Study into Engaging Leadership Practices*. UK: National School of Government, Sunningdale Institute.

Johnson, G., Scholes, K. and Whittington, R. (2006) *Exploring Corporate Strategy*. London: Prentice Hall.

Khan, W. A. (1990) Psychological conditions of personal engagement and disengagement at work. *Academy of Management Journal*, 33(4), 692–724.

Weiss, W. H. (1999) Leadership. *Supervision*, 60(1), 4–10.

Further reading

Department of Health (2009) *The Communicating Organisation: Using Communication to Support the Development of High-Performing Organisations*. Available at: http://www.dh.gov.uk/en/Publicationsandstatistics/Publications/PublicationsPolicyAnd Guidance/DH_110344 [accessed 17 October 2012].

Drucker, P. (1988) More doing than dash. *Wall Street Journal,* 16 January.

Fleming, D. (2001) Narrative leadership: Using the power of stories. *Strategy and Leadership*, 29(4), 34–36.

Goleman, D., Boyatzis, R. E. and McKee, A. (2001) December primal leadership: The hidden driver of great performance. *Harvard Business Review*, Special issue: Breakthrough Leadership, 43–51.

Schneider, B., Macey, W. H., Barbera, K. M., Young S. A. and Lee, W. (2006) *Employee Engagement: Everything you Wanted to Know About Engagement but Were Afraid to Ask*. Rolling Meadows, IL: Valtera.

Snyder, C. R. (2000) *The Handbook of Hope*. San Diego: Academic Press.

Ulrich, D. and Ulrich, W. (2010) *The Why of Work*. New York: McGraw-Hill.

2

Why the emphasis on coaching for organisations?

Janice Steed

Some of the general themes arising in Chapter 1 warrant further consideration. How can we explain the growth of coaching in organisations, and why are organisations relying on and emphasising coaching as an important part of management practice?

Some emerging features of today's Western society

Like most other Western countries, the UK is currently going through huge economic and social instability. This is not just a period of change to be 'got through and then go back to normal', it is a wider change in society which will become the new 'normal'. If we accept this as being the case then it is important to consider what these changes are and how they will affect people and, in turn, organisations.

There are some key differences from the changes and economic downturns of previous decades, which influence the way we are affected and respond as individuals and organisations to the current socio-economic conditions. The first of these is the availability and speed of communication, which brings a paradigm shift to traditional power dynamics and the notion of managers cascading information from 'the top'. While this may still be an expectation for some, there is in fact no necessity for employees to 'wait to be told'.

The second major shift is in the role and position of government or 'those in charge', who, rather than being responsible and accountable for looking after us and therefore in control of the decisions which affect us, are now providing stewardship that enables us to look after ourselves and make our own decisions and choices, in which we have a stake and for which we are accountable. The state is therefore an 'enabler' not a 'controller', with whom we as citizens have a new deal.

The third key area of sociological change is that of the great question of happiness or well-being. What makes us happy and brings well-being? There is now a strong sense that a healthy society needs emotional capability, a shared purpose and a sense of community as well as financial resources to flourish and generate well-being. There is then a great paradox emerging in society, where generating a sense of empowerment and influence for us as employees also creates uncertainty, responsibility and anxiety, all of which are intensely magnified in a world of economic austerity and high expectations.

What does coaching bring?

If we accept that organisations are made of complex human relationships and processes, which are influenced by the wider societal changes within which we live, then we start to see how these sociological changes are mirrored in our experiences at work and in the style of leadership and management we need to reflect these changing conditions. No longer are we required to have all the answers and make all the decisions, but rather we need to create the conditions that allow people to give of their best, to access and develop their own resources, make their own choices and be accountable for their own decisions. This requires managers to be facilitators rather than controllers. It requires a new relationship, a new contract of expectations between parties and a new sense of mutual self-sustainability and support.

Coaching brings a new organisational paradigm in which people are seen in terms of their future potential rather than as resources to be managed – in the way we might think of a machine.

In their book *Freedom and Accountability at Work*, Koestenbaum and Block (2001) describe people as 'walking freedoms', accountable for creating their own world, not passive recipients but active participants in their own, and the organisation's, development and success. This speaks to the very heart of coaching; building self-awareness and enabling people to find the answers themselves through active listening and genuine inquiry. A key part of this is the 'coaching contract' or 'coaching agreement', whereby coach and coachee agree what it is that they wish to work on and how they will work together. Coaching then provides an opportunity for organisations to build another key competency: agreeing mutual expectations through effective communication. When communication is not clear it can be the source of so much conflict.

As with any new relationship there are also challenges in understanding the boundaries and expectations, and coaching requires a level of maturity and self-awareness from both coach and coachee. Ensuring time, a safe place for reflection, and support are also essential qualities of coaching that help build organisational resilience and well-being, enabling individuals and organisations to flex and adapt to the ever increasing psychological, economic and intellectual demands.

Through coaching, people are able to support and harness the best from each other, build trust that can withstand the hard economic realities, and build resilience in times of rapid change. Coaching provides a way of 'being and relating' to each other which offers that organisational resilience and which allows for individual and collective responsibility and growth.

Coaching to improve performance

In *Quiet Leadership*, David Rock (2007), an experienced coach, provides some practical everyday steps to improving performance by transforming the 'organisational dialogue' and modus operandi away from telling people what to do, towards helping them to access their own ideas, energy and insight and to create new thinking by careful listening, effective questioning and belief in their own potential. A fundamental part of this is accentuating the positive, reframing the problem to consider what could be, and then generating solutions in the process. This moves the attention away from dissecting the problem (which can deplete energy and create more problems by concentrating energy on what the problem is) to generating possibilities and forward energy. The simple yet profound premise is that if we can approach all of our organisational interactions (and in particular those between individuals and their managers) in a thoughtful, purposeful way, which uses the best principles of coaching, we can make a dramatic difference to individual experiences and organisational performance as a natural way of being together.

This approach strongly resonates with another positive approach to generating organisational improvement and 'better' states of being – that of 'appreciative inquiry' (Barratt and Fry, 2005). Appreciative inquiry works on the fundamental premise that we can co-create a positive future by building on what is good and works well, rather than focusing on 'fixing the problem'. In so doing, we create energy and commitment and allow for a different conversation with employees, customers and communities at large – what is it that we do well and how can we do more of that? In their article 'Leadership coaching creates every day miracles', Brinar and Decker (2005) show how using this solutions-based approach, as opposed to a problem-solving approach, in coaching can really make a difference to the development of leadership capability across organisations. Drawing on the work of David Cooperrider (2001) and his 'heliotropic hypothesis', Brinar and Decker believe that everyday conversations focus on the negative, and that if we can change this to the positive we open doors to new possibilities and beliefs that we can together share and create momentum towards. This is illustrated in Figure 2.1.

Some of these points and the possibilities that coaching can create are demonstrated in Case Study 2.1, which emerged in the relationship between a hospital CEO and his coach.

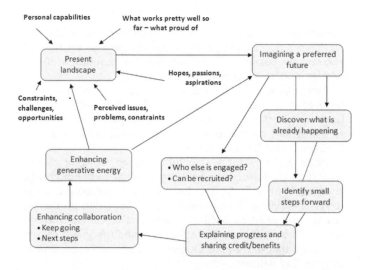

Figure 2.1 Solution-developing cycle (Brinar and Decker, 2005; reproduced courtesy of Ashridge Business School)

Case Study 2.1   The benefits coaching can bring to organisations: An example from the field

Mark is the chief executive of a large teaching hospital in England. He has recently joined the organisation following a difficult period of patchy, and in some places poor, clinical performance coupled with financial difficulties.

Mark feels that the organisation has lost its way, and is no longer concentrating on the core purpose and values of good patient care and clinical outcomes delivered with confidence and compassion, but rather emphasises individual 'fiefdoms'. Mark is keen to change the nature of the patient experience and what people say about the hospital, but more than that he wants to change the nature of the conversation within the hospital to one which is inclusive and values-driven. He wants to find the organisational 'heart', where each and every member of staff feels a personal responsibility and commitment to being different, and feels supported in challenging unacceptable behaviour. He equally feels that this will not be in conflict with the financial position because if people start to work more positively together on building what is best, this will create new possibilities and enhance the reputation of the organisation, so generating more business.

Particularly, he sees that the hospital is not an island unaffected by the wider changes in the NHS and society at large and wants the hospital to be seen as part of the solution to the strains on the local health economy, rather than the problem that is 'bleeding it dry'.

Mark embarks on a structural change, bringing clinical leaders to the fore, but he knows that in itself will not change anything. He needs them to be the 'heart', pumping out the oxygenated blood through the system. In order to do that he realises the need to build capability and resilience, without which old behaviours will easily undermine the 'green shoots of change' that will require a long-term vision and commitment to grow and be sustained.

Mark knows it will be easy to focus on the processes and structures involved in running an organisation but it is this new conversation and way of being which will bring about the real transformation. He draws from his own experience and the benefits he has had and seen in organisations he has worked in before, realising that the best leaders are those who can provide the environment in which others can grow and reach their potential, can ask and find the answers to their questions, and can continue to generate conversations which involve, engage and develop others. He has learned this through coaching and the insights this has brought to him and previous colleagues.

Mark embarks on a courageous path, appointing clinical leaders who are not only prepared to share his vision but also to share the realisation that they need to develop their own self-awareness and ability to facilitate others' development. He then commissions a leadership development programme based on emotional intelligence and coaching.

This combination of workshops, action learning and individual and team coaching, reinforced by organisational transparency of expectations and commitment to conversations about values and purpose (which constantly re-engage with what is it we do best and how do we do more of that) provided the basis for a huge transformation. The hospital is now a place with belief in itself and is believed in by others.

Conclusion

In this chapter we have looked at how the current socio-economic conditions demand new relationships, and how coaching is being used effectively in these circumstances.

Coaching can help to build individual responsibility and commitment and, in turn, build organisational resilience and flexibility to deal with the ever more complex and demanding social context that we now face, and which can no longer rely on top-down, paternalistic leadership models.

Finally, we looked at how coaching can help us access and build the positive resources already present within individuals and organisations; encouraging people to find their own solutions and generate day-to-day conversations, which look at enhancing what is done well, can have a transformative effect on individual and collective performance that will generate impact far beyond the organisation itself.

References

Barrett, F. J. and Fry, R. E. (2005) *Appreciative Inquiry: A Positive Approach to Building Cooperative Capacity*. Chagrin Falls, OH: Taos Institute Publications.

Brinar, W. and Decker, E. (2005) Leadership coaching creates every day miracles: 360°. *The Ashridge Journal*, Autumn, 34.

Cooperrider, D. L. (2001) Why appreciative enquiry? In C. Royal and S. A. Hammond (Eds) *Lessons from the Field: Applying Appreciative inquiry*. Plano, TX: Thin Book Publishing.

Koestenbaum, P. and Block, P. (2001) *Freedom and Accountability at Work*. San Francisco: Jossey-Bass.

Rock, D. (2007) *Quiet Leadership: Six Steps to Transforming Performance at Work*. New York: Harper.

Further reading

Morgan, G. (2006) *Images of Organization*. London: Sage.

3

Building a coaching culture in your organisation

Janice Steed

In his seminal book *Organizational Culture and Leadership* (2004), Edgar Schein describes, through a number of case studies, how culture is formed and deeply embedded through learned and shared experiences. It follows that, if culture is to change, we have first to find out what are the underlying assumptions that have served to sustain individuals and allow them to 'belong to the group'.

These assumptions are often so deep-seated that new members quickly socialise into the norms of the organisation in order to belong. Schein goes on to explain that while the culture may be visible through behaviours and artefacts, and there may be a rational desire to espouse new values, it is not until the underlying assumptions are understood, and the group enabled to see and create new experiences with shared assumptions, that the culture can start to change.

Schein helps us to understand that changing the culture of an organisation is far more difficult to achieve than deciding 'new values'. It requires new ways of 'living out' experiences together, and individuals noticing and taking responsibility for their part in contributing to the existing culture, and their part in creating a new one. This is often extremely frightening as the norms and stabilising features of how to 'belong or even survive' in an organisation start to change, and requires time, commitment and active support. Most importantly, leaders need to model the new behaviours and create a climate that encourages and values the new norms.

Chapters 1 and 2 discussed the external environment and the need for organisations to be flexible and resilient in an ever-challenging and fast-moving world, with individuals being enabled to adapt, move quickly, contribute fully and take responsibility for their own actions. No longer can a top-down, paternalistic organisational model with power vested in just a few individuals hope to serve the needs of the workforce or meet the wide-ranging and fast-changing needs of customers. This is particularly so as competition and expectations increase, and the economic climate becomes more difficult.

In *The Art of Powerful Questions: Catalyzing Insight, Innovation and Action*, Vogt, Brown and Isaacs (2003) make a strong case for organisations and individuals learning how to focus on the right questions, rather than the right answers. This creates a climate of inquiry:

> . . . in order to learn, adapt, and create new knowledge to meet emerging opportunities and challenges in the more fluid organisational structures of the future. For example, the leadership challenges of the next 20 years are likely to revolve around the art of engaging and ener-gising networks rather than solely managing hierarchies as in the past.

However, this is often still at odds with our experiences at work, where command and control, personal power and tribalism can be writ large. Recognising these patterns, why they exist and what might serve the organisation better within this wider societal environment is a critical first step to building a coaching culture.

The benefits of a coaching culture

So why a coaching culture and what does that look like? A coaching culture encourages openness, inquiry and reflection through questions, challenge and support. It enables every-one to 'help others to help themselves', through structured conversations, constructive challenge, inquiring behaviours and the belief that everyone can achieve their potential if they are given the opportunity to develop personal awareness and insight and to generate their own solutions. As John Whitmore (2009) states when referring to Timothy Gallwey: 'Coaching is unlocking people's potential to maximise their own performance'; the distinction being in enabling self-development from within, rather than teaching from outside.

In building a coaching culture it is certainly important to first ascertain the nature of the current organisational culture and, drawing on Schein's work, be clear about the beliefs and values underlying 'how things are done around here'. What are the espoused beliefs, values and behaviours and what are the experienced beliefs, values and behaviours? It will be important to understand this in order to then consider what difference a coaching culture can make and how great a distance may have to be travelled.

Leading the way: the importance of leadership

One approach would be to establish inquiry teams across the organisation who, through semi-structured interviews with 'peer departments', could explore how it feels to work in the organisation. By gathering stories and creating a picture of the shared assumptions and what is important to people, and asking the important questions about the beliefs and values that underpin shared assumptions, it is possible to generate a dialogue about whether they still serve us well or if there is something better that we could create together.

An important part of the success of such an approach will be in the climate that is created by senior leaders and middle management. Is it safe to explore and be encouraged to ask questions about the current culture, how well it is working and for what purpose? Often, it is most impactful to build on positive elements of where things work well. 'Where are we creating good results and feedback from our customers?' Sometimes, it will take the realisation that we need to change to survive, and that the best solutions lie from within, harnessing the talent and ideas that we have, rather than searching for them somewhere else.

In his book *Good to Great*, Jim Collins (2001) considers the best companies develop from within, with what he refers to as 'level 5 leadership' – 'humble and ferocious', where leaders are concerned with the good of the company more than their own personal success. A leader interested in the good of the company, who has an ethos of 'your success is my success' and 'the company's success is our success' will, in turn, be able to see the benefits of coaching – creating possibilities for individuals and teams to reflect, grow and learn, find their own solutions and challenge the status quo in pursuit of the greater good of the organisation.

Building a coaching culture

Building a coaching culture through modelling and leadership style is essential. In his article 'Awakening authenticity', Kevin Cashman (2003) describes the power of the 'leader-coach', who explores and awakens possibilities rather than offers advice or gives solutions, and thus generates commitment and energy. Appraisal processes, operational working arrangements, such as project teams and one-to-one relationship building, and a culture of empowering and enabling individuals to seek out the answers, inquire, constructively challenge and support, all help to create the norms of a coaching culture.

A coaching mindset requires managers in particular to give up the notion that they need to have all the answers and that their way is the best or the only way. They need to have the humility and confidence to help individuals work things out for themselves. Individuals equally need to take hold of the opportunity and the personal responsibility they have been given to create their own solutions, and to live with a greater degree of uncertainty as different ideas and ways of doing things are explored.

Coaching also provides the opportunity to build a culture of mutual support and the ability to challenge from a position of shared organisational interest in how individuals can contribute fully to the organisation, rather than the divisive, destructive behaviours which exist in organisations and are based on competition and blame; where individuals protect their own self-interest, often at the cost of wider organisational success.

In such situations, however, individuals, when encouraged and through changing their own behaviour, can start to generate novelty and difference just by behaving differently with their colleagues and teams – making the 'difference that makes the difference' as described by Adrian McLean and Kevin Power (2007) when discussing the work of Gregory Bateson in their article 'Framing Bateson'.

In her article 'Radical change the quiet way', Deborah Myerson (2001) describes a number of examples where change can happen through individuals behaving differently and, through their own actions, making an impact on the prevailing culture. Case Study 3.1 shows how a senior manager did just that, changing the culture within the organisation by working differently with her team and demonstrating very different results, which then started to spread throughout the organisation.

Case Study 3.1   Changing the culture within the organisation

Amanda is head of midwifery in a small district hospital. She joined the hospital about a year ago and found herself presented with a number of serious incidents and a demoralised and dysfunctional service with a long history of difficulties and a poor reputation with the public.

Amanda had known about some of the difficulties before joining; however, she had not appreciated the extent of the history or of the pervasiveness of the culture within the hospital as a whole. As a midwife, Amanda is acutely aware of the importance a positive, confident experience has on the outcomes for a woman's pregnancy and birth, which can leave a lifelong impact on her and her family. She also knows that in order to provide such experiences she needs to have positive and confident staff, and that the dysfunctional situation that is now deeply embedded is at the heart of the problems the service is now facing.

One of Amanda's big difficulties is that the wider culture in the hospital is aggressive and dictatorial, with an 'attribute blame and just fix the problem' type of environment that had grown up with the previous chief executive and leadership team, creating a climate of fear and self-protection. However, a new chief executive has recently been appointed following the serious incidents in the maternity services, and Amanda is hopeful that she may be able to demonstrate that a different management style is possible and can achieve far greater performance.

Amanda is very aware and alert to understanding that people's experiences need to change if she is going to make a change to day-to-day beliefs and behaviours. As such, she starts to go about things very differently. She listens, and begins to address some of the fundamental issues over recruitment, education and environment. She encourages conversation and questions rather than dictating what should be done. She commissions a 'reflective review of maternity services', which involves over 50 individuals and groups within and outside of the unit being involved in semi-structured inquiry interviews. They share their stories in confidence and categorise the themes that emerge into: 'how things are around here', what are our beliefs and assumptions, where do they come from, what do we (or I) do as part of that, what would we like to do differently and how will we create that?

Through this process individuals start to see the culture within which they are working and more importantly they start to see their part in that. There is catharsis in sharing their individual stories while creating energy and confidence through the development of a new meta-story of how they wish to be in the future, with Amanda being able to reinforce that confidence through her own modelling of behaviours and expectations from herself and the team. Further, through this process Amanda is able to widen her understanding and commitment to her medical and managerial colleagues, enabling a wider ripple impact beyond the individual disciplinary level and creating a shared team approach essential to the maternity service. They commit to the following areas in creating this new culture:

- Acknowledging the story and moving on, with clear messages and modelling from the top with respect to culture and behaviours – changing the story of 'how we do things around here' using multi-disciplinary appreciative inquiry-based projects to 'look out and bring in' positive solutions and build on the best of what happens now.

- Development of the maternity leadership team with a shared vision and ways of working by demonstrating positive leadership which encourages inquiry.
- Clinical leadership development and internal facilitation on a day-to-day level of multi-disciplinary team working, using complaints and serious incidents as well as positive experiences to reflect together on ways of working.
- Using stories as a way of sharing experiences, especially experiences from women and their families.

This process has been underway for only a few months now, but Amanda is already seeing a transformation in the unit's reputation and the experiences of its users; the retention rate of staff has hugely improved, and the overall performance and quality indicators are improving each month. The unit is now receiving attention for the right reasons, and a sense of pride rather than shame is starting to build. This is also having an impact on the rest of the hospital; the new chief executive has noticed and is promoting a different way of working. Bullying and blame, being told what to do and when to do it, are no longer just accepted as the only way of doing things.

Despite the early positive signs, Amanda is not naive; she realises that the culture which has been so embedded in individuals who are scarred and lacking in confidence will not change overnight, and could easily slip back into the old patterns.

She is therefore aware that working alongside staff, giving a balance of support and challenge, building their confidence and experiences on a day-to-day level, needs to be sustained over the longer term. As such, she is careful to ensure she maintains her own support mechanisms and continues to use a coach herself and a strong, supportive network of other midwives. She has also ensured that her own team have access to individual support, again modelling this in her leadership as a positive feature and not something that is regarded as remedial action.

Amanda has recently presented to the board, who are now considering a wider reflective review and an organisation development programme to develop a performance-enhancing culture.

Conclusion

In this chapter we have considered the nature of culture and how that is co-created within organisations, with a significant influence from the leader, which is then reinforced through the leadership–followership relationships in the organisation.

We have looked specifically at some of the elements of a coaching culture and its benefits; a culture which promotes inquiry with a sense of shared influence, responsibility and commitment, together with support and challenge.

Finally, we have looked at identifying the features of the current culture, bringing to the fore its underlying beliefs and assumptions as a way of supporting and bringing about cultural change in order to build a healthier coaching culture which is more inclusive and generates shared commitment and responsibility in the organisation.

References

Cashman, K. (2003) Awakening authenticity. *Executive Excellence*, 20(5), 5–7.

Collins, J. (2001) *Good to Great*. London: Random House Business Books.

McLean, A. and Power, K. (2007) Framing Bateson. In B. Critchley, J. Higgins and K. King (Eds) *Organisational Consulting: A Relational Perspective: Theories and Stories from the Field*. London: Middlesex University Press.

Myerson, D. (2001) Radical change the quiet way. *Harvard Business Review*, October, 35–41.

Schein, E. H. (2004) *Organizational Culture and Leadership*. San Francisco: Jossey-Bass.

Vogt, E., Brown, J. and Isaacs, D. (2003) *The Art of Powerful Questions: Catalyzing Insight, Innovation and Action.* Mill Valley, CA: Whole Systems Association.

Whitmore, J. (2009) *Coaching for Performance: GROWing human potential and purpose.* London: Nicholas Brealey Publishing.

4

The journey towards a coaching culture

Deborah Fleming

Organisational culture plays a critical role in creating an environment where employees are engaged, committed and supported during a transformation or change initiative. This chapter presents a case for using a series of 'levers' for change in an attempt to increase organisational effectiveness (of which coaching is a part) rather than implementing coaching *per se*. This argument is supported by case studies of two private sector clients, who have had different organisational outcomes from their investment in coaching.

I propose that a coaching culture does not happen by 'doing' coaching. A tailored suite of actions is recommended to implement a culture of coaching, which in turn, directly contributes towards achieving organisational transformation and facilitates a positive, creative and rewarding working environment. Some isolated interventions can have limited impact on the bottom line and may not contribute directly to organisational effectiveness. There are four key questions I will answer that are linked to the journey towards a coaching culture:

1 Why has there been an increasing trend towards favouring a coaching culture?
2 What defines a culture of coaching?
3 How does a coaching culture affect organisational change?
4 What hinders coaching becoming part of a culture?

Why has there been an increasing trend towards favouring a coaching culture?

In order to answer this question, one needs to describe the context that a typical organisation is currently facing. This is likely to include the following:

- Leaders with a multitude of initiatives to manage (at the same time).
- Employees with little time to embed change.
- High levels of fear and loss from change/restructuring.
- High levels of ambiguity – particularly around basic hierarchies of need.
- Leaders lacking time and space for creativity; favouring task over relationships.
- Cost cutting of a magnitude not experienced in the last decade.
- Reduction in the presence of two-way feedback and affirmation to build confidence in employees and let them have a say in direction.

It is fair to conclude that coaching can 'raise the bar' for individual performance during these testing times in organisations. Through constructive feedback and reflection, coaching can enrich individual learning experiences. For leaders, gaining the benefit of regular time and space that the discipline of coaching provides can bring a reduction in stress. The benefits of coaching are all well documented, and are discussed in other chapters of the book.

The increasing trend towards favouring a culture of coaching is final acceptance of the limitations of coaching in isolation. Organisations now want things on a bigger scale, at a sharper pace, in a deeper form and with higher market impact. Customer needs are greater and the market stakes are higher. Coaching a leader as an isolated intervention does not necessarily help an organisation grow, change and adapt at a pace and scale that the current context demands. The focus in this chapter is therefore on the debate between coaching versus coaching as part of a transformation programme.

What defines a culture of coaching?

Case Study 4.1 shows how a large organisation successfully embraced a coaching culture.

Case Study 4.1   Coaching as a cultural shift – a suite of coaching elements

In 2009, a global petrochemicals company asked for consultation to support a transformation programme to reduce costs through relocation and selling off two areas of the business. The department involved was the biggest contributor of profit in the global business (over $110 million). The cultural incentive was to see, act and behave differently with customers, listening more actively to their needs rather than promoting themselves as experts and specialists. The 'expert' behaviour had historically made the organisation's reputation strong in the marketplace, but with new competition from China and offshore organisations, behaving in a more collaborative way with customers was defined as competition beating. The leaders' 'expert' advice-giving had also impacted employees by making them highly dependent on instruction from leaders before initiating a task.

The organisational development consultants set up a programme of interventions to measure the existing culture and to get a clear understanding of what had made the organisation successful up to that point. They used a series of psychometric tools called Organisational Culture Inventory (OCI) and Organisational Effectiveness Inventory (OEI)[1] to give insight into what the future culture should look like. Findings from the OCI and OEI were as follows:

- Leaders' behaviour was 'solution focused', 'task driven' and innovative.
- Leaders set ambitious direction for the organisation and monitored results closely.
- Employee findings, however, differed starkly, stating low levels of loyalty, fatigue and lack of recognition or feedback.
- High levels of dependence on leaders had been bred over the years by providing answers to employees' challenges.

- Ideas were not heard or listened to owing to the lack of time or space to think or reflect on learning, and there was a fear of giving upward feedback. This was impacting levels of innovation in employees.

One senior manager at the time stated: 'if we are impacting our employees in this way, our customers will inevitably see the signs, so we need to reset our behaviours and accept that what has helped us so far may hinder our onward growth.' Indeed, customers cited the need for more partners in their solutions, not experts.

A number of levers for change were planned:

- *Make the link between a coaching style of leadership and the core strategy*
- Without a change of behaviour and increased awareness of patterns and norms at the top of the organisation the new direction would not work. A series of workshops were held with the senior team to build the case for change in behaviour by viewing real data and feedback from employees and customers, and by analysing market data/ share. This involved a 'team coach' presenting the leaders with a 'reality check' and giving them quantitative feedback. This was the driving force behind making the link between leader behaviour and strategy.

- *Give leaders time and space to reflect on feedback and build their skills in giving and receiving it*
- Feedback can be received defensively when loss of control and power are at stake in organisational change. Having an 'expert' coach to model giving feedback is a helpful way to gain acceptance behind change. Use of 360-degree feedback tools has a part to play here in closing the gap between leaders' perceptions and the reality of their behaviour. This was a method used in this case.

- *Put a process in place to incorporate regular employee 'upward' and 'downward' communication*
- Leaders may get better at giving feedback following a variety of learning initiatives (see previous point) but the key success lies in their employees feeling that they can give

feedback upwards and be heard. These interventions ranged from 'brown bag lunches', 'town halls', 'team huddles', blogs and webcasts, where leaders actively asked for advice from employees at the 'coal-face' of the challenges. The consistent and aligned communication, channelled two-way in the organisation, supported employees in feeling safer to ask customers what they thought rather than defaulting to leader intervention. It also allowed leaders to manage the volume of information. The communication strategy focused almost entirely on removing barriers to organisational learning and managing information overload during change, as noted by Brown (1998, p. 101): 'Limitations are most obviously exposed when individuals are faced with highly interconnected, fast-changing and complex environments, which overload people with what can seem ambiguous, confused and contradictory messages'.

- *Coach individuals to adapt to new culture*
- Different personality types reported different challenges with 'letting go' of the old culture and embracing the new one of seeing the customer as expert, listening more, and *asking* instead of *telling*. Here, the one-to-one coaching of executives and key 'change champions' was vital to success. The tailored support provided from a coach provided the time, space and challenge to practice a change in behaviour in a safe place. Here, psychometrics like the Myers-Briggs Type Indicator® (MBTI®)[2] have a role in building self-awareness and confidence.

- *Coach change teams; building and using their diversity of thinking*
- Business psychology has a role to play at a team level in supporting change teams to challenge the status quo, or to build stability (depending on the stage of change in the organisation). An example here was the behaviour in team meetings of debate, debate, debate and 'yes, but . . . no, but . . .' challenge. A memorable (and rather brave!) intervention in one meeting was for the business psychologist and team coach to interject with: 'I am observing the love of debating the challenge rather than deciding the outcome.' These sort of process interventions come from externally trained and

trusted coaches who are helpfully observing what a team is not yet noticing. Culture resides more in the collective relationships than it does in individuals. Individual development will not, by itself, shift the culture. Another relevant team coach observation was to notice the team's predisposition to enjoy change, due mainly to the combined MBTI 'NT'/ 'NF' personality types in the team (Intuitive Thinking/ Intuitive Feeling – people who enjoy long-term vision and logic or longer term vision and relationships), when the relevant stage of change required a focus on *stabilising* the environment. 'TE' (Extroverted Thinking) and 'NE' (Extroverted Intuitive) personality types enjoy critiquing the future possibilities and are quick to see the big picture when faced with change. They focus on what is next and scan horizons for ideas and possibilities. These particular personality preferences can sometimes make them repeat change for change's sake. The MBTI was a tool used successfully in this stage.

- *Set quick wins and affirm people*
- Small achievements on a project Gantt chart can be huge psychological achievements for people in the organisation. The change team set out early on to identify quick wins (even having an enormous colourful timeline in the office entrance hall) and each time an achievement was made ensured that people knew about it. The positive atmosphere and appreciation of contributions made people feel generally less overwhelmed by the scale of the changes that were being made. This coaching technique was key to moving the culture from one of critiquing and debating to collaborating.

How does a coaching culture impact organisational change?

In Case Study 4.1, the outcomes from the series of organisational development and coaching interventions were that the cultural shift was less painful for the people involved: 'We were treated as individuals', cyclical patterns of thinking and learning were challenged quicker, and collectively at the top, and modelling behaviours was possible on a scale that individual coaching would not have impacted as forthrightly.

Attention was focused on 'business as usual' while the organisation developed the new behaviours needed to 'let go' of being expert. The diversity of thinking styles in the organisation was quickly tapped into through psychological analysis rather than hunch. This saved valuable time and allowed a focus on the positive aspects of loss with leaders.

Feedback from customers became habit rather than a one-off annual gesture, and competition with Chinese markets became more focused. Two-way feedback also built trust in the organisation, and the customer became the 'expert'.

What hinders coaching becoming part of a culture?

In stark contrast to Case Study 4.1, Case Study 4.2 describes the unsuccessful adoption of a coaching culture.

Case Study 4.2   Coaching a group of leaders – a single layer of coaching

In 2010 a large global retail client engaged coaches in an effort to become more forthright and brave in its leadership style. It was widely recognised that tough market conditions, lack of recognition and high levels of competitiveness were impacting confidence in its leaders. Quarterly offsite meetings were the token method for reflecting, and stress was high. A new HR initiative for leaders was launched and its focus became to 'create and maintain space' and 'have more conviction in your decisions'.

External executive coaches were selected to work individually with senior leaders, with the standard remit to bring confidence and conviction back into the leaders' belief systems. Coaching itself was seen as the space needed to help leaders. The coaches were collectively briefed to understand the organisational system in which the leaders operated and all coaches were immersed in a period of induction to understand the retail environment at that time – yet they would ultimately have limited impact on changing it!

Sponsorship from the client was high and contracting at the outset was strong, with processes in place for feeding back the non-confidential themes from the coaching to the sponsor to aid future performance. Metrics were agreed and leaders began the coaching with a three-way meeting with the coach and their regional retail leader.

Rich data/themes became available to the coaching organisation in the form of lack of time and space to think, burnout in the leaders, high rates of cancellation at the last minute, feelings among the leaders of being 'disconnected' from their head office, and pressure to 'meet the numbers'. Through supervision, it became apparent that, at a subconscious level, the coach's role had became one of helping the leader to survive within the organisation, but not change it. Changing coachees' own behaviour ultimately had limitations at an organisational level, while the struggle internally became about financial results, not personal results.

In one memorable review session, a leader who had completed coaching shared her progress in feeling more confident in herself; more able to challenge, learn and manage stakeholders more effectively. In turn, the coach reported to the sponsor that the leader had demonstrated high levels of commitment to the coaching, zero cancellations, high levels of personal risk, and learning. This progress was only to be measured by the sponsor in a different way when they disclosed that the leader in question had just received a low performance rating based on target, and was likely to be sidelined.

Conclusion

The learning in taking two separate organisations on a coaching journey was significant for me. Both experiences had success in building self-awareness, confidence, meeting objectives and delivering increased performance. The data gained from non-confidential coaching themes were fed back to the sponsor and acted upon.

However, in Case Study 4.1 (the petrochemical example), dramatic results were gained by the influence of the coach at the top of the organisation, and also from the coach becoming a (temporary) member of the change team. Some of the following advantages were realised:

- The ability for the coach to observe the leader *in situ* in the influential groups shaping and changing the culture of the new organisation as it developed.
- Tightly managed boundaries between executive coach and team coach meant that quantitative and qualitative data were acted on strategically.
- Safety was constantly managed and supported by the coach from within the organisation as the culture developed.
- The coach was able to manage any dependence the leaders had on them, which psychodynamically gave insight that the old culture of dependence on the focus of authority was still prevailing.

In Case Study 4.2 (the retail client), the culture of the organisation remained focused on performance and 'making the target' throughout the duration of the coaching. The ability of coachees to influence upwards and shape culture was limited to the coaching evaluation feedback forms and sponsor review. Coachees did not necessarily have role models back in the organisation who practised 'creating time and space to reflect', so their own reflection time (in the form of the coaching) was often challenged, with coaching sessions being cancelled citing 'pressures of work'.

As the coach in both the case studies, I personally gained rich data from being a legitimate and accepted part of the system in the petrochemicals organisation and was able to use my own feelings (and frustrations) to understand the dynamic in the culture in which the coachees were slowly changing. I learnt that a carefully crafted suite of interventions (e.g. communications strategy, team coaching, culture inventories, 360-degree feedback), all meant that common failures of change programmes, like lack of engagement, were avoided and that coaching became a vital part of the levers for change, but not the only lever.

Notes

1   Human Synergistics® International. http://www.humansyn.co.uk.
2   CPP Inc. http://www.cpp.com.

References

Brown, A. (1998) *Organisational Culture*. London: Pitman Publishing.

Further reading

Barger, N. J. and Kirby, L. K. (1995) *The Challenge of Change in Organisations*. Palo Alto, CA: Davies-Black Publishing.
Colenso, M. (2000) *Successful Organisational Change*. London: Prentice Hall.
Harvey, D. (2001) *An Experiential Approach to Organisational Development*. Upper Saddle River, NJ: Prentice Hall.
O'Mahoney, J. (2010) *Management Consultancy*. Oxford: Oxford University Press.

5

Why some leaders and managers are reluctant to be coached

Mary Joyce

The subject of why some leaders and managers are reluctant to be coached is more complex than it at first appears. What does a 'reluctant' leader or manager look like, and how is this reluctance both manifested and understood? Surely, someone who is reluctant to be coached will make sure they are not a recipient of coaching! In some cases this is true, and we can only speculate about the reasons for their reluctance, but there is another group who do experience reluctance at the prospect of working with a coach, and for whom it is difficult to decline the offer of coaching. This may be because it is part of a leadership development programme, part of an organisation-wide initiative to foster particular behaviours, or for other reasons of this kind, where there is an expectation (possibly from a higher authority) that the leader or manager will be coached.

The issue for consideration in the chapter title could be interpreted as suggesting that a reluctance to be coached is something that is difficult to understand, because there is an underlying assumption that coaching is an enriching, positive and enabling experience. The many testimonies to the effectiveness of coaching often describe it in terms of helping people make change happen, revealing surprising insights that alter self-image, and which consequently effect behaviour change. So why might this not be desirable, and how can a reluctance to be coached be explained? A good place to begin is with a clearer idea of what is meant by 'reluctance' and how it is different from, but related to, the concept of 'resistance'.

We may define reluctance as an unwillingness to engage in a course of action – in this case, being coached. We may not be persuaded that it is the right solution or may have some doubts about it but, whatever the reason, it results in an ambivalence which does not necessarily prevent the coaching taking place but means the motivation to make it work and enter into a good working alliance with the coach will not be there at the outset of the work. There is, however, held within the notion of reluctance, a potential space for change, where further information or experience could enable a shift to occur from an initial 'unwillingness' to be coached into a 'willing' engagement with coaching. A 'resistance' to coaching is, by comparison, a more defined and active refusal to comply with the expectation or proposal to be coached, and the potential for a creative exchange between coach and coachee that could result in a shift towards a more involved engagement is therefore less likely. The phenomena of reluctance and resistance can be evident at conscious and unconscious levels, and can be understood as part of the architecture of defence mechanisms.

This prompts questions for the coach around whether someone who is reluctant to be coached can be helped, whether the proposed coaching model is the most suitable for them, and the most effective ways of working with them if the coaching is to achieve results. This will be considered later in the chapter.

Although the use of coaching in organisations has increased in recent years, there are still widely different views on what it is, and whom it is for. The extremes of these divergent views are represented at one end of the spectrum by organisations in which coaching is seen as an investment in the leader or manager, maybe as part of a proactive talent management strategy, and where it acquires the kudos of other benefits accessed by senior executives or those singled out for fast-track development and promotion. At the other end of this continuum, coaching can be seen and experienced as remedial; a solution to a problem with an individual whose behaviour or performance needs to be 'fixed'. It is therefore not surprising to find that the way in which the organisation views and makes use of this intervention is likely to have some impact on the mindset of the person who is to receive coaching.

In the first of these examples, an individual who is offered coaching might view it as an affirmation of their worth and a positive demonstration of how the organisation recognises their talent, values their skills and abilities, and is prepared to invest in them by providing coaching to help them advance further in their career and in the organisation. In the second example, the individual offered coaching would know that a coach is only used when something goes wrong, and when there is a problem that needs to be fixed. Although coaching in this example is an offer of help, it may bring individuals into contact with a view of themselves that causes them to feel anxious about their position and career prospects within the organisation. It may also be the vehicle for providing feedback to the individual on aspects of their behaviour or performance that have not been disclosed to them before by colleagues or their manager. The individual in a situation such as this may enter coaching reluctantly, viewing it as the equivalent of a very long examination they will need to 'pass' in order to move out of the HR spotlight and return to a more secure place when it is over, where there will be less scrutiny and analysis of their behaviour and actions.

We can see, in the two examples outlined above, that the key to understanding why some managers and leaders are reluctant to be coached lies in understanding their reluctance as a conscious or unconscious response to something in the organisational culture, and/or something that is linked more closely to their internal emotional and psychological state of mind. Whichever it is, in their reluctance to be coached the manager or leader is engaged in a form of withdrawal and is protecting themselves against an internal (psychological) and/or external (organisational) threat. The response therefore needs to be understood in the particular context of the individual's organisational culture and both their level of and capacity for self-awareness and reflection.

Coaching, reluctance and organisational culture

In contrast to the examples illustrated, there are organisations where coaching is used as part of a strategic HR intervention and has its place in an organisational culture where feedback and learning are part of the leadership and management styles practised. Individuals are likely to be very active and interested in their personal development, and will expect to be involved in a continuous process of self-reflection in the context of reviewing how they are performing, what they are able to achieve, and how they might develop themselves further to support their work. Coaching might be something they request for themselves, and within the organisation it will be used and experienced as a positive way of supporting growth and development, and of tackling problems. For organisations operating in this way there is a level of trust and a partnership with employees that makes it possible to create the conditions for coaching to be effective. Coachees will have confidence in the contracting arrangements, feel secure about confidentiality and reporting protocols, and will be motivated to make coaching a successful support for their work.

Other organisations operate in different ways and have different values, and the culture may produce a markedly different response to coaching. If a bullying and blame culture exists, and colleagues and leaders are not trusted, there may not be sufficient safety for individuals to feel secure enough to be coached. If the suggestion of coaching comes from a manager or a colleague in HR it may be regarded as suspicious – is there an ulterior motive, is this a way of 'checking up' on them, or part of a covert plan to get rid of them? The reality of the offer of coaching may of course be different, but whether it is perceived as a helpful or suspicious offer will depend on whatever is happening in the organisation at the time, the dynamics of power, and its culture. In a situation that is not felt to be safe, reluctance and/or resistance would be a response by the individual to protect themselves from a perceived threat or danger as part of a survival strategy that allows them to keep working in the organisation until a change occurs that removes the source of danger. If the individual were to contract a coach in a private capacity it would remove the external cause of fear associated with the organisation providing the coaching, though not necessarily result in the individual feeling secure enough within themselves to confront their work situation and explore their options; deferral becomes another part of the survival strategy.

Coaching, reluctance and personal mastery

The situations described so far demonstrate how the external environment can impact on an individual's attitude and response to coaching. But it is also possible for an individual to be reluctant to be coached in a 'coaching-friendly' organisation. The reasons for this are likely to stem from a fear of what might be uncovered in the coaching – in other words, the threat is an internal one to the individual, and defence mechanisms are triggered to protect them from a conflict that may be felt as anxiety, emotional pain or discomfort. I have borrowed Peter Senge's term 'personal mastery' to describe the presence or absence of a level of self-knowledge and openness that comes from a commitment to inquire at a deeper level into understanding self and others as part of complex systems, so that it becomes a discipline:.

> *When personal mastery becomes a discipline – an activity we integrate into our lives – it embodies two underlying movements. The first is continually clarifying what is important to us . . . The second is continually learning how to see current reality more clearly . . . People with a high level of personal mastery live in a continual learning mode. They never 'arrive' . . . [they] are acutely aware of their ignorance, their incompetence, their growth areas.*
> (Senge, 1990, p. 141)

When Senge refers here to a 'discipline' that embodies two movements, we can see that it requires an individual to be self-aware and capable of shifting their attention from within themselves to what lies outside in the environment and back again, calibrating their perception and understanding accordingly as they make sense of their situation and choose their response.

Coaching is intended to increase self-awareness in support of growth and change and, whatever the model used, necessitates some reflection on one's actions, purpose and relationships with others. As a process, coaching involves addressing some deep questions and learning about oneself through the relationship with the coach. For some leaders and managers this may be a particularly difficult prospect because it requires them to accept a state of 'not knowing' in order to explore what can be known and learned. If their daily lived experience of being a leader and manager is always one of being looked to for answers and certainty, with the expectation that they will know more and have specialist knowledge that others do not possess, it may be very uncomfortable to give up the mantle of omniscience in order to place themselves consciously in a place of not knowing. It also means that leaders and managers would need to be able to acknowledge their feelings of vulnerability; something that may neither be expected nor approved of in their daily work role.

For Chris Argyris, managers and leaders represent a group of highly intelligent and 'smart' people, for whom self-reflective learning poses a particularly difficult challenge. In 'Teaching smart people how to learn', Argyris (1991, p. 2) identifies leaders and managers as examples of educated professionals who are often very good at a problem-solving approach to learning but when the solutions fail they are less able to engage in 'double-loop' learning, which requires a more critical look at their own behaviour and actions:

> *Solving problems is important. But if learning is to persist, managers and employees must also look inward. They need to reflect critically on their own behaviour, identify the ways they often inadvertently contribute to the organisation's problems, and then change how they act.*

Argyris is describing a way of thinking and acting that comes from developing the capacity for reflection, so that intention and action can be more congruent. It relies on the individual increasing their level of self-awareness and being capable of exploring their fears of being wrong, making mistakes, failing, not measuring up to expectations and, para-doxically, their fear of learning. Argyris observes: 'We learn to create defensive routines early in our lives. As adults, we help foster organisational climates that support these routines. The cycle becomes self-reinforcing' (Keller Johnson, 2005).

These unconscious defensive routines are ingrained, block learning and lead to blame or fault being attributed to others, so that the leader or manager is protected from having to take responsibility for their part in what is not working or has gone wrong. The opportunities to learn from failure, fear and disappointment are likely to provide the conditions for achieving a level of introspection that confronts and ques-tions a way of thinking and its underlying assumptions, so that a deeper understanding of organisational problems and issues is possible. While coaching is an effective way of exposing these defensive routines so that learning can be made available, this may be the very outcome that the leader or manager is reluctant to face.

Coaching reluctant leaders and managers

Elisabet Engellau is a clinical professor of management at INSEAD, and writes of her early experience of being an executive coach (Engellau, 2007). She describes the coaching assignment she had with the new CEO (David) of a US retail business. The coaching contract had been made by the vice president of HR, who thought it a good idea to provide coaching support for David in his transition phase as the new CEO. David went along with the arrangement but turned out to be a reluctant and resistant coachee, with a strategy to hold his coach at 'arms length':

It did not take me very long to realise that my effective-ness as a coach was extremely limited. I wondered whether he viewed me as a spy who was reporting every-thing to the [vice president of] HR . . . whenever David and I met, both of us seemed to go through the motions, knowing that we were expected to do something, but not doing much about it.

(Engellau, 2007, p. 242)

Not long into his term as CEO David was fired, having received a pay rise only weeks earlier and a congratulatory letter; he was left shocked and angry. He had not expected this outcome, nor seen any signs that it might be a possibility; his coach was similarly surprised. Three years later they met by chance and David was able to tell Elisabet, his former coach, that he had only realised much later that he had been in an organisation that was not 'right' for him.

Engellau's paper is an instructive and fascinating account of working with a resistant leader and learning from 'failure' (her words), or maybe more accurately, how to do things differently in the light of experience. It demonstrates the capacity and willingness of the coach to reflect critically on her part in David's coaching journey and learn from the experience, and underlines the rich opportunities (and discomfort) that 'failure' and mistakes provide for learning:

> *I have sometimes heard colleagues in the leadership coaching business say that failure is good; it is the 'fertiliser'. Everything they have learned about coaching, they have learned from mistakes. And they might be right. After all, if you are not making mistakes, you are not doing anything. I made many mistakes in the David case, but it was also a great learning experience for me.*
> (Engellau, 2007, p. 254)

But this account also raises the question of why David resisted his coaching. Freud (1895, p. 117) wrote of 'the blindness of the seeing eye', where one knows and does not know something simultaneously – a psychic process that creates a distance between us and experiences that we prefer to be kept out of our awareness. This is part of the defensive mechanisms referred to earlier and, in this example, David is not aware of how he is perceived by his senior colleagues, does not 'read' the signals about the transition to CEO in the company and, consequently, is neither able to 'calibrate' his response to the situation he is in nor use the resource he has in his coach. However, even though David was a resistant leader in coaching, the work he was able to do with his coach seemed to provide him with something much later on in his life and career that he could use to help him learn from, and make sense of, his experience. What he learned was important in terms of recognising the type of organisation within which he could be effective and happy.

Conclusions

What conclusions can be drawn from this exploration of reluctance and resistance to coaching? There are coaching professionals who advise against working with reluctant coachees and conclude that the coaching cannot be successful if there is not a willingness to be coached and a positive attitude on the part of the coachee. I prefer to work with the idea that something might happen to change an initial reluctance into something more positive – and to regard coaching as offering that 'potential' space. There may be many reasons for leaders and managers to be reluctant coachees, but it is important to understand their reluctance and to explore and acknowledge it rather than avoid or oppose it. This is the learning that Engellau takes from her experience; she refers to this approach as 'resistance judo', a term taken from family therapy and meaning 'going with the flow; using the opponent's momentum to one's advantage'. Working with a coachee's conscious or unconscious resistance can give them a space within which to experiment, test out their fears and be understood. Between the coach and the coachee is a creative space, full of potential and undetermined:

> *Between stimulus and response, there is a space. In that space lies our freedom and power to choose our response. In our response lies our growth and our happiness.*
>
> (Covey, 2004, p. 65)

References

Argyris, C. (1991) Teaching smart people how to learn. *Harvard Business Review*, May–June, 1991, 99–109.

Covey, S. (2004) Foreword. In A. Pattakos, *Prisoners of Our Thoughts: Viktor Frankl's Principles for Discovering Meaning in Life*. San Francisco: Berrett-Koehler.

Engellau, E. (2007) The dos and don'ts of coaching: Key lessons I learned as an executive coach. In M. F. Kets de Vries, K. Korotov and E. Florent-Treacy (Eds) *Coach and Couch*. New York: Palgrave.

Freud, S. (1895) *Studies on Hysteria*. Standard Edition (Vol. II). London: Hogarth Press.

Keller Johnson, L. (2005) Combating defensive reasoning. *Harvard Management Update*, March 2005, 3–4.

Senge, P. (1990) *The Fifth Discipline*. London: Random House.

Further reading

Amado, G. (2009) Potential space: The threatened source of individual and collective creativity. In B. Sievers (Ed.) *Psychoanalytic Studies of Organizations*. London: Karnac.

Amado, G. (2009) Psychic imprisonment and its release within organisations and working relationships: OPUS Conference, London, 21–22 November 2008. *Organisational and Social Dynamics*, 9(1), 1–20.

Armstrong, D. (2005) *Organisation in the Mind*. London: Karnac.

Brunning, H. and Perini, M. (Eds) (2010) *Psychoanalytic Perspectives on a Turbulent World*. London: Karnac.

Harvard Business Review (2004) *Coaching and Mentoring*. Boston: Harvard Business School Press.

Kets de Vries, M. (2011) *Reflections on Groups and Organisations*. West Sussex, UK: John Wiley and Sons.

Pattakos, A. (2004) *Prisoners of our Thoughts: Viktor Frankl's Principles for Discovering Meaning in Life*. San Francisco: Berrett-Koehler.

Peltier, B. (2010) *The Psychology of Executive Coaching*. East Sussex, UK: Routledge.

O'Neill, M. B. (2007) *Coaching with Backbone and Heart*. San Francisco: John Wiley and Sons.

Sievers, B. et al. (2009) *Psychoanalytic Studies of Organisations*. London: Karnac.

6

Encouraging managers
to coach their colleagues

Gwen Wileman

*Line managers have a crucial role to play in people
management and development and the line manager as
coach role is increasingly being advocated as an important part of line managers' responsibilities.*

(Chartered Institute of Personnel
and Development, 2009)

Why should managers coach their colleagues?

This chapter considers how managers can be encouraged to
coach their colleagues and to see this as a positive and natural
management style for them as an individual. The need to
communicate and demonstrate clear business and personal
benefits that the manager can relate to is critical. An exploration of the culture, support mechanisms and benefits of
coaching is the theme of this chapter, with a focus on the key
steps needed to equip and encourage managers to engage in
a positive way and see the value in it for themselves and their
team.

Many line managers make use of coaching skills in their
day-to-day relationships with their teams and colleagues. By
building on these skills and providing a supportive environment, organisations can help line managers increase their
awareness of how they can improve the performance of their
people and achieve business goals more effectively. Coaching
by managers can be relatively informal, and it is wise not to
overcomplicate the process. Coaching in this context is best

presented as just one more skill in the manager's toolkit, building on what already works for them in terms of engaging, motivating and managing their staff.

Encouraging line managers to adopt a coaching management style is more likely to be successful if it is seen by top management as a business issue rather than a learning and development department initiative.

> *While coaching skills may be part of a line manager's toolkit, it may be inappropriate to expect the deep rapport, level of confidentiality and boundary management expected from formal coaching relationships. The line manager as coach role is better understood as a coaching style of management, integrated within a move from a 'command and control' approach to a more participative style of management.*
>
> (Chartered Institute of Personnel and Development, 2009)

The report from which this quote is taken, *Coaching at the Sharp End: The Role of Line Managers in Coaching at Work*, is an important piece of research that assesses the devolution of coaching to line managers and examines coaching from the perspective of the line manager. The report highlights the importance of dealing with potential obstacles as well as ensuring an enabling and supportive environment.

The 2010 Chartered Institute of Personnel and Development (CIPD) *Learning and Talent Development Survey* reported that the most effective learning and talent development practices, as perceived by the responding organisations, are in-house development programmes (56 per cent in 2009 compared with 48 per cent in 2008) and coaching by line managers (51 per cent compared with 47 per cent). Coaching by line managers has increased in 56 per cent of the organisations surveyed in the last two years.

The need to encourage line managers and support them in developing and improving their coaching style of management has never been so critical. This chapter offers a simple approach that identifies the three practical steps necessary to encourage managers to see coaching as a highly positive tool for them to achieve improved business performance (Figure 6.1).

Figure 6.1 **The three practical steps**

- *Step 1* Raise awareness of the benefits: What's in it for me?
- *Step 2* Equip managers with skills and confidence: How do I know I am doing it well?
- *Step 3* Develop a supportive organisational culture: Is coaching valued?

Step 1 Raise awareness of the benefits: What's in it for me?

What will motivate managers to be prepared to 'give it a go' if they are new to coaching or to develop their skills further if they already feel comfortable with a coaching style? The simple answer is because they can see potential benefits for them in their day-to-day activity of achieving high performance through their people.

For many managers a pivotal part of their role is to improve individual performance; arguably this can most effectively be achieved by a coaching approach. To be successful and deliver the best results this activity needs to take place in a supportive coaching culture.

It is critical to make managers aware of the kinds of situations when coaching opportunities may arise so that they can be prepared to seize these in a positive way. Coaching opportunities are often simply not recognised until it is too late. In their book *Making Coaching Work*, Clutterbuck and Megginson (2005) suggest a 15-point checklist which I believe provides a useful (if not exhaustive) starting point to encourage managers to coach their colleagues:

1   When a new project or assignment is given.
2   When an error has been made.
3   When a new member joins the team.
4   When there is feedback (from any source).
5   When there is conflict between members of the team or between the team and outsiders.
6   When people feel a lack of confidence.
7   When the team is in danger of becoming complacent.
8   As a result of regular development reviews, either team or individual.
9   When there is a change in technology or business process.
10   Where inappropriate, inadequate or dysfunctional behaviour is observed.
11   When targets are missed.
12   When individuals or the team wish to raise their game.
13   When people feel they are operating too much in a 'coasting' mode and need to be stretched more.
14   When one person acquires a skill that could be helpful to others.
15   When organisational politics intrude.

Every manager will be facing some of these issues at any one time, and the trick is to raise managers' awareness that each 'challenge' offers an opportunity to coach towards a solution.

Clarifying the role of manager as coach

It is important to be clear about the role of a coach in your organisation – some organisations (see Case Study 6.1) outline a definition up front, which can be helpful so that managers understand what is expected of them.

The role of managers in coaching can vary across organisations and there tend to be three broad distinctions. Managers need to understand these. First, manager as coach, when managers are equipped with coaching skills and are then encouraged to adopt an informal coaching approach with their staff. This is the main area of focus for this chapter. Second, managers may be involved in supporting the coaching process if a member of their team is receiving external coaching, or third, they may be trained as an internal coach and be involved in coaching others outside of their team.

Martin Howe (2008) argues that 'although the tackling of under achievement and skills development provided by "operational" coaching can be extremely helpful and may produce a number of performance related benefits, line managers cannot provide the transformational coaching needed for sustained strategic and cultural change.' This needs additional organisational input. Line managers need to understand where they fit and should be seen as important contributors, alongside internal and external coaches, to the journey towards transformation.

Understanding the boundaries

It is important to recognise the psychological boundary issues for line managers. Many professionals identify that the roles and responsibilities of line management make formally coaching your own staff very difficult. This is often owing to the challenge of developing a deep rapport with all team members, reluctance of team members to share personal issues when that may be seen as a weakness, and availability of quality time. Clutterbuck and Megginson (2005) found that coaching behaviours were often abandoned in the face of more urgent, if less important, demands on managers' time. However, it is clear that much benefit is gained by supporting a coaching 'style' in line management and many organisations are investing in this, often alongside their internal or external coaching systems. Finally, it is important to ensure that managers are aware of when coaching is not appropriate. For example, a major crisis calls for clear direction and action, not coaching!

Step 2   Equip managers with skills and confidence: How do I know I am doing it well?

Make sure initial coaching training is practical, relevant and produces immediate results that managers can use as examples and share with one another.

Coaching training is best done using real situations for coaching conversations, rather than role play, as this is likely to help managers develop their coaching skills confidently in a safe environment. Think about the coaching skills line managers currently have, how to build and develop them and how to use them most effectively; for example, skills such as active listening, open questioning, summarising and reframing. The training should also provide an introduction to one or more simple coaching processes, such as the GROW model (Whitmore, 2002) to provide an appropriate framework to work with.

The issue of sustainability is important; how to ensure managers continue to review their progress, further develop their skills and become much more confident in using a coaching style. Ideally, the initial training should be short (no more than one or two days) then bring the coaches back together again to review progress and share and learn from successes. There is a real opportunity at this stage to highlight successes and note any tangible returns on investment.

Ongoing communication about how coaching has made a difference is important. Ask staff to provide examples of how this type of coaching has increased their motivation, morale and results. Staff surveys are a useful way of doing this. Ongoing networking to share tips and techniques can be an important support mechanism for individuals embarking on coaching, but also a way of developing a coaching culture across the organisation. Enthusiasm for coaching in organisations often develops virtually by word of mouth; the case study examples in this chapter demonstrate the impact of this.

Case Study 6.1 is an example of a structured, strategically focused introduction of a coaching initiative for managers in a large further education college. The approach to training in this case included the key elements outlined in

Step 2. The key to its success were the senior leadership commitment to this change process and individual managers' willingness to make coaching central to their own management approach.

Case Study 6.1   Doncaster College: manager as coach – a new approach

Doncaster College is a large further education college with 1,100 staff and around 20,000 students. The college has embarked on a very structured three-year programme of developing around 70 managers with the skills and confidence to operate a coaching style. This programme is firmly driven by the strategic priorities and core values of the college and indeed, in itself, is a way of embedding them. For example, the coaching programme is aligned with the core value 'mutual support and understanding'.

The programme includes two one-day non-accredited skills development workshops for 70 managers, with planned coaching practice between modules. External coaching is available for the most senior managers, and a complementary management skills programme is running alongside the coaching programme. In addition, ten individuals will be selected to be further trained and developed on an Institute of Leadership and Management Level 3 coaching qualification to provide an 'internal coach' to support the ongoing culture change programme at the college. The long-term objective is transformational; to build sustainable, high-quality management and leadership capacity and changes in attitudes and behaviour. The specific characteristics and benefits of the programme have been documented as outcomes and these will be used to assess the impact of the coaching programme.

A definition of what coaching means in the Doncaster context and the specific benefits and characteristics were agreed along with the investment. In three years' time the return on that investment will be measured.

There are a number of ways in which managers at the college have been encouraged to buy into the programme and its subsequent outcomes. One of the most important is the role modelling and support of the college principal, who sees this as fundamental to the culture change and improved performance of the college. He has personally participated in the coaching training programme and vocalises his support for a coaching style on a daily basis.

Time has been ring-fenced for the training to emphasise its importance, peer coaching activity has been introduced and is increasing, and the most senior leaders are being coached personally by external coaches and have become champions. The coach training also breaks down barriers and encourages knowledge sharing. This is an enormous benefit and is often a direct outcome of peer coaching relationships.

Finally, by linking coaching firmly into the needs of the business and embedding it into the culture of the college, it is seen as being intrinsic to organisational success. This, more than anything, is what gives managers the confidence to participate in the change.

Ongoing support for internal coaches

As well as coach training at an appropriate level there is an ongoing need for managers to meet with like-minded people and seek advice, guidance, new insights and inputs to improve their coaching. The approach at Warwick University Coaching Network (Case Study 6.2) is well developed and includes a wide range of staff at the university who coach as part of their work, including academic staff, professional staff and staff developers.

Case Study 6.2   Warwick University Coaching Network

The Warwick Coaching and Mentoring Network is open to staff at the university. Its aim is to create partnerships, outside the normal line management relationship, where one person helps another to enhance their performance, learning or development.

The Warwick Coaching Network is a group of members of staff at the university who use coaching in some aspects of their work. The group meets once or twice a year, generally for half a day followed by lunch. The group has two main purposes. First, as the name indicates, it is a network that provides an opportunity for staff with a working interest in coaching to make contact with one another and hear how they are using coaching in their practice. Members of the network come from different parts of the university, such as the careers service, the Business School, the Medical School and the Institute of Education, and include members of the staff development unit. This leads to a sharing of ideas and sometimes to collaborative endeavours. For instance, contacts made through the network led to the Medical School and the Institute of Education working together to develop a postgraduate award in coaching and mentoring.

Second, the group is a community of practice. A member might bring along a model or approach that they use in their work and share this with others, generally by inviting them to engage experientially with the material. More recently, the network has held a number of coaching masterclasses. The first looked at solution-focused coaching and cognitive behavioural coaching, and considered how members might incorporate ideas from these two areas in their work. A second masterclass explored approaches sitting towards the non-directive end of the coaching spectrum, such as clean language and motivational interviewing.

As well as these two main purposes, one of the benefits felt by members of the network is a sense of support and affirmation for their work and the place of coaching within it. It is heartening to engage with like-minded folk who believe in the value of coaching and who want to extend their coaching capabilities.

(Bob Thomson, Learning and Development Adviser, Warwick University)

De Haan and Burger (2006) provide some very practical guidance on peer coaching. Professionals today have an increasing need for lifelong learning and much of their continuing professional development takes place through interaction with peers and colleagues; it is often done without planning and often by accident. De Haan offers a framework to better organise, supervise and facilitate professional development through peer coaching. This can be a valuable approach to the ongoing development and support of coach managers and is a useful reference for organisations willing to encourage the development of peer coaching in their organisation.

Step 3   Develop a supportive organisational culture: Is coaching valued?

Managers will be more motivated to embrace a coaching style if they believe that they and the organisation will benefit, and that their efforts will be rewarded and recognised. The best way to encourage managers comes from demonstrating that coaching is in their best interests and for them to see the benefits for themselves. They will then share this experience with colleagues and begin to generate a bottom-up approach to a developing a coaching culture.

'A coaching culture is one where coaching is the predominant style of managing and working together, and where a commitment to grow the organisation is embedded in a parallel commitment to grow the people in the organisation' (Clutterbuck and Megginson, 2005). This is the ideal environment in which to encourage coaching, although most organisations have yet to reach the stage of progress that Clutterbuck and Megginson (2005) refer to as an 'embedded' coaching culture. This is a difficult journey for organisations and takes time. It can succeed only if obstacles such as cynicism, time and resource constraints, and perceived lack of skills and confidence are addressed.

In encouraging managers to coach their colleagues it is necessary to listen to their concerns, gain their buy-in and identify champions. Do not try to impose from above but recognise the other challenges a line manager faces and work with them to realise the benefits for them and the organisation.

Case Study 6.3 outlines how a supportive coaching culture was introduced into a university.

Case Study 6.3   De Montfort University: an emergent coaching culture

Provision of coaching by an experienced internal coach was the initial catalyst for the development of a coaching culture in a large, successful, city-centre, post-1992 university. At that stage the perception of the value of coaching was that it was either remedial (only available to poor performers) or elitist (only available, externally, to senior leaders in the organisation).

Over the next two years the word spread; coaching successes became the topic of corridor conversation among managers and the volume of demand increased very significantly. A wider group of willing volunteers were trained as internal coaches, in particular HR partners who had an important role as organisational 'coach and conscience'. They were in a privileged position to be accepted as coaches (without the title) to managers in handling people management issues in the faculties and departments across the university. This helped demonstrate potential benefits.

At no time was a specific coaching skills programme launched; the skills were learned as part of general management training and development focused on dealing with specific and very relevant people management aspects of a manager's role.

At this stage the experienced internal coach won a national excellence award for his approach and this raised the profile of a coaching style of management as a positive and well-regarded approach. Managers became more interested and wanted to find out more!

This case study is a good example of an organic and emergent coaching culture (Knights and Poppleton, 2008) where variation in coaching practice is accepted and uniformity is not seen as a key issue in different parts of the organisation. It was not seen as a top-down initiative but as a more subtle, reinforced and aligned approach that in time gathered its own momentum and was driven by the managers as they saw and recognised the benefits in their day-to-day work. From this we can learn that to introduce and embed coaching slowly at first can result in a 'pull' approach that gathers its own momentum.

Conclusions

- Managers are more likely to be convinced that coaching is the tool for them if they hear colleagues talking about how it has made a difference to them, their team or their department. They need to believe it is in their own best interests.
- Ensure managers are equipped with the requisite skills and do not underestimate the lack of confidence managers might feel in coaching, even when trained. They need to practise, get feedback and understand there will be no negative consequences. Motivated managers feel they are capable of coaching effectively.
- A welcoming and supportive coaching culture is important if coaching behaviours are to become embedded in the organisation. This can take time and determination.

References

Chartered Institute of Personnel and Development (2009) *Coaching at the Sharp End: The Role of Line Managers in Coaching at Work*. London: CIPD. Available at: http://www.cipd.co.uk/hr-resources/practical-tools.

Chartered Institute of Personnel and Development (2010) *Learning and Talent Development Survey*. London: CIPD. Available at: http://www.cipd.co.uk/hr-resources/survey-reports/default.aspx.

Clutterbuck, D. and Megginson, D. (2005) *Making Coaching Work: Creating a Coaching Culture*. London: CIPD.

De Haan, E. and Burger, Y. (2006) *Coaching With Colleagues: An Action Guide to Peer Consultation*. Basingstoke: Palgrave Macmillan.

Howe, M. (2008) Coaching at the crossroads: Is it enough to position coaching activity with line managers? In *Coaching and Buying*

Coaching Services. London: CIPD. Available at: http://www.cipd.
co.uk/hr-resources/guides.

Knights, A. and Poppleton, A. (2008) *Developing Coaching Capability in Organisations*. London: CIPD.

Whitmore, J. (2002) *Coaching for Performance: GROWing Human Potential and Purpose* (4th ed.). London: Nicholas Brealey.

Further reading

Chartered Institute of Personnel and Development (2008) *Coaching and Buying Coaching Services*. London: CIPD. Available at: http://www.cipd.co.uk/hr-resources/guides.

Chartered Institute of Personnel and Development (2007) *Coaching in Organisations*. London: CIPD. Available at: http://www.cipd.
co.uk/hr-resources/research.

7

Dealing with more complex coaching incidents and knowing when to hand on to someone else

Mary Joyce

This chapter explores some of the circumstances that can arise in coaching when it may be in the best interests of the coachee to refer them to another professional. The roles of the internal and external coach are considered in this context, as are the differences between coaching and therapeutic support as a response to the issues that can arise when coaching a client, and where additional professional support might be necessary and helpful. The chapter discusses the importance of professional supervision for the coach, and uses a case study to demonstrate how a diagnostic framework can help clarify the decision points where further help and support might be sought. Sources of further information and referral agencies are provided at the end of the chapter.

Complex coaching incidents

The term 'complex coaching incidents' is used in this chapter to refer to situations where the focus of the work undertaken with a coachee reaches a point where it becomes intractable; where the initial need expressed in the request for coaching takes on another dimension that requires a more intense form of professional support, for example from a psycho-therapeutic and/or medical practitioner. We start here with a consideration of the structural complexities that arise in connection with the role of the internal coach, and their potential impact on the coaching relationship.

The internal coach: the use of coaching in organisations

As we have seen in the previous chapters, many organisations in both the public and private sectors are now using coaching as part of their in-house professional development offer to staff, recognising that it can be a powerful way of increasing individual and organisational performance and of supporting change. There are different practices among organisations in how they make coaching available to their staff and how well informed they are about the range of coaching models in use and their relative strengths. Many choose to provide some or all of their coaching through members of staff who take on the role of 'internal' coach in the organisation. This has many advantages and can be incorporated into a broader practice of peer learning, with benefits accruing from the creation of a dynamic learning culture which supports learning and feedback as key processes in contributing to a more emotionally intelligent workplace. Within this organisational practice the internal coach must also work with the constraints this places on the coaching relationship, because the coach shares an organisational context with peers or colleagues.

The nature of these shared relationships and culture raises the issue of objectivity and independence, and can contribute to the complexity of the coaching situation; for example, where an external coaching intervention or other professional support may need to be considered for the coachee. Levels of training may also be a secondary and limiting factor for some internal coaches working with more challenging coaching relationships. We will consider some of these circumstances and how to deal with them, as well as paying attention to the ways in which they define the 'edges' of the work of the internal coach.

The internal coach: a systems perspective

It is sometimes assumed that there is little difference between coaching that is delivered and practised inside the organisation and that provided by an external coach. However, one of the most important and fundamental differences is that the internal coach is likely to perform their role as coach alongside or as part of a more formal role in the organisational structure, in which they will have a set of relationships that are defined by levels of power, responsibility, accountability and authority. They will have in common with their coachee some of the inside knowledge of that organisation and its culture, and possibly shared relationships. In this way, the coaching relationship is located within the organisational system and is part of an interrelated and complex set of structured relationships. The diagram in Figure 7.1 is a spatial representation of the positions in the organisational system occupied by the internal and external coaches in relation to their coachee.

The roles of the internal and external coach are considered and discussed more fully by Erik de Haan (2008,

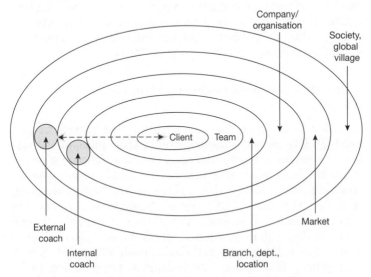

Figure 7.1 **The coach and coachee in the organisational system**

p. 16), who argues that these structural positions explain why the internal coach cannot be truly independent of the organisation. This should not be interpreted as meaning that the internal coach does not hold to a professional code of ethics or that they are in some way less able than those who practise outside the organisation. Instead, it draws attention to the positions occupied by coach and coachee within a shared system, and how this is an important factor in the way they conduct and experience their coaching relationship.

The internal coach will have their own experience of what it is like to be in the organisation, and will be closer and more connected than an external coach to some of the situations and people described by their coachee. This may be explained by conceiving the organisational system as 'carried inside' both the coach and coachee, and internalised – like a fractal or hologram. As they work in and share this same system, the coach may find it difficult to be truly objective in listening to their coachee. There may also be particular issues that could make it difficult for the coachee to feel completely safe and be confident about confidentiality (e.g. promotion prospects, fear of contract termination, bullying, harassment and/or performance anxiety). Again, none of these factors relate specifically to the personal qualities of the internal coach – they arise because of the boundary position both individuals occupy within the organisation.

Managing complex coaching situations: boundaries

In order to mitigate these constraints, the internal coach needs to give careful consideration to their place in the system in relation to a potential coachee and anticipate whether there are likely to be other factors that could compromise the coaching work. Using the organisational system diagram (Figure 7.1) gives a clear sense of the degrees of separation between coach and coachee; the greater the space between them in the system, the more emotional and psychological space there is likely to be in the relationship for their work to take place. This allows the contact between them to be managed through good boundaries; for example, thinking about whether there is a sufficient organisational boundary in place to help the coaching work, as manifested in the coach and coachee coming from different departments, locations or management structures, and any other considerations that could impact on their relationship.

Attending to these points at the outset will make it easier for the coach and coachee to manage the more personal disclosures or vulnerabilities that might surface in their work together.

The external coach by comparison does not carry the organisation of the coachee within themselves in the same way. They are likely to hold a vantage point which is separate and kept apart from the daily work life experienced by their coachee. From this position they are likely to observe different things because their vision is freed from a shared daily experience of the organisation. Their points of reference will also be different, especially if they practise as coaches in a range of different organisations.

It could be argued that these factors present additional challenges for the internal coach, in that they need to attend constantly to how the shared system is affecting their judgement and their response to their coachee. If they are working in a toxic or dysfunctional organisation it may also be harder for the internal coach to look after their own emotional and psychological health, with so little space between themselves, their coachees and the organisation (see Kets de Vries, 2006, and Maccoby, 2007). This is discussed later in the context of professional supervision (see 'The importance of professional supervision', p. 76).

It may appear at this point in the chapter that the internal coach is at a considerable disadvantage. However, there are some advantages for the internal coach. They will have a good knowledge of the organisation; the political, market and sectoral context of the coachee's work; and the scale of their relationships. They may also be able to pinpoint more quickly the issues that need attention or are being avoided. This shared context can generate a faster development of trust and rapport because the coachee feels understood in their working context.

The boundary between coaching and therapy

The focus for coaching in the workplace is usually on achieving specific results and outcomes. This may be helping the coachee develop skills or deepen their understanding of some aspect of their work so that they have more conscious choices available to them for thought and action; for example, how they deal with conflict in their relationships or manage themselves more effectively in a situation of change and transition. In this sense we could say that the coaching relationship, at its best, makes it possible for the coachee to look at themselves and their relationships in a broader context of the organisation and its purpose, and as part of a dynamic process.

Consequently, they are able to reflect on what they are seeing and learning about themselves, as experienced through the coaching relationship, in order to achieve a better integration between what they feel and think, and how they behave. This could be further supported and informed by data such as 360-degree feedback results and psychometric assessments.

The change experienced by the coachee can be transformational and, although the focus is primarily on 'work', it can have a positive impact upon other areas of the person's life. It is therefore important to have in view the ways in which the roles we hold in life are interrelated and connected, and how change in one area of our lives can affect the other parts. It is not surprising then, that as the coachee becomes more aware of their 'blind spots', the coaching relationship and process may touch on more personal areas and emotions not usually disclosed to colleagues. This can be a very emotional and cathartic experience, and although it is to be expected it can also uncover more complex underlying issues and dynamics not yet recognised or anticipated by the coachee at this point in the coaching relationship.

These situations are likely to be difficult because they occupy the boundary between coaching and therapy. The more extreme examples of the continuum are those where the coachee is experiencing a level of physical and/or emotional distress which dominates to the extent that the organisational focus in the coaching work is lost temporarily or shifts permanently.[1] This situation requires a reassessment with the coachee of their needs, and may require a more intense level of support in the form of a medical or therapeutic referral.

There is much that coaching and therapy have in common but they are also quite different in focus and practice, as are the training and personal development requirements for each of these practitioner roles.[2] The challenge for the coach (internal or external) is in developing a 'good enough' understanding of where the boundary lies, and having good judgement of the work in progress with their coachee and whether it is progressing within the boundary domain of coaching.

Developing good judgement

In coaching work it is helpful for the coach to have a sense of the emotional life of organisations and to be psychologically aware; this includes being self-aware and paying attention to their own professional development. A coach uses this capacity in working with their coachee, and it is exercised when more complex coaching situations arise. It is tempting to focus on the coachee at this point and to concentrate on describing the aspects of behaviour that might be classified as 'difficult', as if these were clearly observable stand-alone indicators on a checklist. Whatever the behaviour, it arises and is expressed in the relationship with the coach and needs to be interpreted within an understanding of what has been happening in the coaching relationship. Knowing when there is a problem, and that it should be dealt with by someone else, is likely to be something that the coach is able to identify and assess if they have developed their capacity to pay attention to what they are feeling when they are with their coachee.

This is an important piece of intelligence, sometimes referred to as the 'transference'. Important signs in a complex coaching situation might be where the coach feels uneasy at the prospect of being with the coachee, overwhelmed, not able to connect with them, or where they feel out of their depth or there is a non-specific anxiety. Again, these are examples of when the coach can make use of their own experience of being with their coachee to help interpret and assess what might be happening with them. If the coachee repeatedly misses sessions, is repeatedly late or rearranges sessions, what is being communicated apart from the surface-level explanation? These are important signifiers of something that needs to be understood at a deeper level of inquiry so that it can be used either to further the coaching work or identify sources of additional, or more appropriate, professional support for the coachee.

The importance of professional supervision

Whether a coach practises as an internal or external coach, it is vital they have access to regular professional supervision; this is part of good practice for any professional coach. Supervision provides the professional space for the coach to reflect on their coaching practice with a suitable professional in a confidential setting where they can discuss their practice and any concerns they have about their work with coachees. This can take the form of one-to-one or group supervision – the latter has the added benefit of learning with peers and gaining insights from shared practice. This is of particular value for internal coaches, and provides the support needed to think about more complex coaching situations as they arise, and how to deal with them. It can be especially useful if the supervisor has clinical training and has experience of dealing with more severe psychological conditions, such as forms of depression, relationship difficulties etc., and is able to help the coach think about the extent to which these might be limiting conditions for coaching.

Clearly, people's personalities and life histories are in play alongside the roles they have and express at work, and these may be touched upon in coaching; for example, a lack of confidence in taking up a new work role may be linked to an early family experience, and it may be important to make this connection explicit in order to be able to work on strategies to increase the coachee's confidence in their new role. It is, however, also possible to imagine a point where this example of a lack of confidence tips over into a discussion where the focus changes and the conversation is no longer predominantly about performing a work role, but covers a more complicated and deep-seated range of difficulties relating to self-esteem. Unless these difficulties are dealt with in a clinical setting, the coaching is unlikely to reach a point where further progress can be made.

Bruce Peltier (2010, p. xxxvi) cites a recent Harvard survey of executive coaches, which concluded that because some executives had mental health problems, coaches should have had some training on mental health issues in order to be able to recognise common 'psychopathologies'. The study goes on to say that coaching was found to be unsuccessful when coachees were 'unwilling to look inward'. Examples of behaviour presented by the executives in their coaching sessions, and identified as being particularly resistant, were linked to narcissism, deep resentment, a sense of resignation and 'very serious self-esteem issues' (p. xxxvii). These are examples of coaching situations that could be considered suitable for referral to psychotherapy.

But perhaps the most significant aspect of the behaviour described above is that the coachees do not appear to have the capacity to reflect on themselves and their internal emotional world. Without reflection on action (the work of Senge and Argyris; see Chapter 5) change is not possible.

The resistance of the executives in the Harvard survey to work with the behaviour they present at a conscious and unconscious level results in their being unable to use the coaching support available to them. This too is a useful indicator for the coach of reaching a point in the coaching relationship where a different form of professional help may be necessary to achieve the objectives articulated in the coaching contract (e.g. behaviour change).

Again, it is tempting to list a description of pathological behaviours that fall neatly into the domain for therapy, as distinct from the behaviour and range of issues that might properly be addressed in a coaching relationship. As we have seen, interpreting all the data in the context of working with a coachee is important in developing an assessment, but this non-specific advice may also appear less than helpful in practice.

Diagnosing complex coaching situations: a way forward

A possible way forward is to build on the overarching framework developed by John Heron (1975) for describing the range of interventions that take place between practitioner and client. Applying this to the particular context of coaching, the work that can take place in a productive and effective coaching relationship has an 'enabling role'. One of its most significant features in 'intention' and 'purpose' is as a 'catalytic intervention':

> *I would say that in general terms the catalytic category has a key functional role. It is the lynchpin of any practitioner service that sees itself as fundamentally educational in the widest sense of encouraging the client's power in living, learning and growing.*
>
> (Heron, 1975, p. 8)

When coupled with viewing the coachee as a 'person-in-role', this approach allows us to work in a more fluid way, recognising the overlapping dimensions in the coaching relationship of the person (personality and life history), their role (the skills and attributes they bring to the job they do and its functions) and their place within a wider organisational system and its dynamics. This perspective is demonstrated in the work of Halina Brunning (2006, pp. 132–6), who uses these dimensions to construct a diagnostic framework to provide the foundations for her model of (executive) coaching (Figure 7.2).

Brunning identifies six domains through which the different dimensions of a person's life can be understood and 'mapped', along with the linkages between them and how they affect each other. Each domain offers a dominant 'lens' through which the lived experience of the coachee can be viewed and explored. These domains are also linked to a professional area of practice, with coaching as the central intervention and anchor point for the discipline and practice of the coach. The domains connect to coaching, but a dominance of attention in the life story and personality domains could signal that psychotherapy or counselling might be more

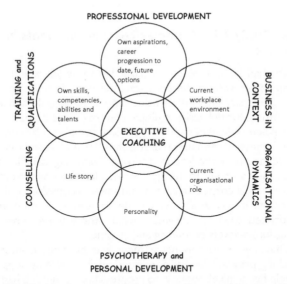

Figure 7.2 **The six-domain model of executive coaching in action (Brunning, 2006)**

appropriate interventions for addressing the issues arising from this area. The model is useful as a diagnostic support to help find a focus for the work with the coachee at the outset of coaching, but also as part of an ongoing 'working framework' to test the focus of the work as it progresses, and whether it is still aligned with the purpose and intention of the coaching contract. The framework can give focus to the data discussed earlier and can be helpful in assessing whether a referral to another professional is appropriate.

Complex coaching incidents in practice

Case Study 7.1 can be used to demonstrate how the model can be applied in practice, and also picks up on a number of themes discussed in the chapter so far. In this example, an internal coach is coaching a colleague in her organisation; during the course of their work together, more complex issues come to the surface and further professional help is sought by the coachee.

Case Study 7.1   Complex coaching incidents in practice

Sandra had been a middle manager for three years and held a demanding role in the corporate services directorate in a large university. She led a small team of four people and was responsible for delivering multiple complex projects, each one with exacting timelines and budgets. Sandra had regular contact with the internal and external stakeholders involved with each project and took the lead in resolving and managing difficulties when they arose in the project work. Her team had projects with external corporate clients, and she was conscious of how important it was to achieve and deliver the work they were contracted to do in a climate where there were concerns about future levels of funding and income.

The university's HR department was piloting an internal coaching programme, and Sandra asked for coaching support to help her think about how to progress her career. She had no previous experience of working with a coach but thought it would be helpful to talk to someone who knew the university and might be able to share some ideas about how she could move forward in her career.

The first session began with the issue that Sandra brought to the coaching contract. She wanted to talk about the work she was doing, the opportunities for progression and how she might start planning to put these ideas into action. Although this is what Sandra said she wanted help with, her coach reflected on the session afterwards and felt that the session had been characterised by a circularity of questions and answers that had not produced much for the work they were to do together. She had experienced Sandra as 'hard to reach' and like a 'tightly bound ball of wool'.

In the sessions following this, her coach encouraged Sandra to talk in a freer way about how she experienced her role, team and work in the university, and what she felt her achievements had been in the three years since her promotion. These discussions focused in on the detail of her current day-to-day experience of her role and revealed how frustrated and beleaguered she felt with her work. She described not being able to achieve anything in her work and how her team and colleagues were 'useless' because they could not do anything for themselves and relied on her to do everything, being seemingly unable to use their initiative and get on with things without her intervention.

In one of these sessions, Sandra's coach decided to share with her the observation that Sandra seemed to be trying to do everyone's job, as well as her own, and how responsible she seemed to feel for everyone. This was a critical moment in the coaching journey for Sandra and her coach because it led Sandra to make a connection between this experience and the role she played in her family. Sandra's earliest memories were of her mother's chronic illness, the impact it had on their emotional and physical needs, and how she had taken her mother's place in looking after the family. Sandra was distressed and tearful in recalling these events and found it difficult to continue – as if she had come to a stop. Her coach asked whether she had ever had any professional help in working through these early experiences, and suggested that she might find it helpful to talk to a counsellor or psychotherapist to explore these past experiences and the impact they might be having on her present life.

Sandra said she wanted to suspend her coaching and take some time away from work. In this time she found a psychotherapist and began treatment. She returned to work and told her coach she wanted to continue coaching but focus on how she could behave differently in role. Sandra and her coach re-contracted and their work together continued in parallel with her private psychotherapy. This intervention seemed to have the effect of 'liberating' the coaching work, so that Sandra was able to focus on experimenting with her role. She seemed less fearful of doing this and was able to let go of her need to be in control of everyone's work. She received very positive feedback from her colleagues and team, who told her that they felt better able to contribute and that she listened to them and trusted them more to do their work. As a consequence, she was managing herself better in her role and was better able to use the coaching support that was available to her in her organisation.

Analysis of the case study

The following observations emerge from Case Study 7.1:

- Using Brunning's model, we can see that Sandra's request for help is in the domain of career aspirations (professional development) but shifts into her current workplace and role (business in context), where the information about her mother's long-term chronic illness shifts the focus again into the life story (counselling) domain. The model tracks the development of the coaching conversation in a helpful way, in that it signals a point for consideration and decision for Sandra's coach. Although Sandra's career aspirations and work role were uppermost at the start of the coaching, they moved into a more subordinate focus for the coaching work as it progressed.
- The coach is able to make use of her own feelings and impressions of the coachee 'in the moment' to notice that something is not quite right – Sandra is experienced by her coach as being 'like a tight ball of wool'. Through guiding her to talk more freely about her work, the coach enabled Sandra to make an important connection between one part of her life and another, and how it was adversely affecting her work role.
- We can see the coach working with a focus on enabling Sandra to grow and develop in her organisation and be more effective in the role she takes up, while also noticing that Sandra's early experience in her family is highly significant and is now showing up in the domain of psychotherapy and counselling.
- The coach is confident about her role as coach, the focus of the coaching and the limits of her skills. She acts with great sensitivity and care in raising the issue of counselling with Sandra. She does not 'prescribe' therapy for her, but through asking the question of whether Sandra has had counselling in the past is able to take forward an open discussion about seeking therapeutic support, enabling Sandra to make a decision about what she wants to do with this new realisation and insight.
- As the coach is internal to the organisation, the management of Sandra's more detailed personal history may be

experienced as more 'containing' for Sandra if it is held outside of the coaching relationship and the organisation.

• The introduction of psychotherapeutic support for Sandra seems to 'liberate' the coaching when it resumes, and sharpens its focus. She has a separate place where she is able to address her early family experiences and their consequences, and a more focused space in her coaching relationship to look at how she can transfer the new knowledge and understanding she is gaining about herself to her working practice. The mutually supporting effects of both interventions running in parallel are evident in the feedback Sandra receives from her colleagues.

In the case study presented here, we can see that Sandra has the capacity to recognise that she needs therapeutic help with the issues uncovered in coaching. She gives herself some time to start therapy and is then in a position to know that resuming her coaching will complement and support the work she is undertaking with her therapist; she recognises the separate and distinct domains of coaching and therapy. While in this particular case the outcome is good, it is as well for the coach to be prepared for less satisfactory endings when coaching issues are on the boundary with therapy. Although a therapeutic intervention may appear to be the most appropriate form of support and help for a coachee, it may not be something they either want or are able to pursue.

Conclusions

The courage and internal resources required of the client to seek and accept psychotherapy should not be underestimated. For some, the prospect of entering into a (possibly lengthy) process with a therapist may be experienced as the equivalent of 'digging up the drains', and may be too frightening and disturbing to contemplate. In situations like this, professional supervision will be invaluable for the coach to think through whether a form of 'boundaried' support is appropriate and can be provided for the coachee, and what its duration should be, so that both coach and coachee are served well by the work within the constraints and possibilities of the situation.

Coaches with a well-developed network will have access to colleagues who work in clinical settings, and will have some local knowledge and experience of the work of reputable psychotherapists and counsellors who may be available to work with coachees who decide they want to enter into psychotherapy or counselling. There are also several national organisations that provide helpful information and guidance on the types of therapy available, examples of the conditions suitable for treatment and how to find a qualified psychotherapist. Some of these also provide a book list for those who want to find out more before seeking treatment. The web sites of these organisations are listed under 'Further reading'.

Notes

1   Examples might be physiological symptoms of stress such as sleeplessness, loss of appetite, panic attacks, acute anxiety, skin and gastric complaints.
2   See Peltier, B. (2010), *The Psychology of Executive Coaching*, East Sussex, Routledge, p. xxxix for a more detailed comparison of the practice and focus of coaching and therapeutic work and coaching.

References

Brunning, H. (2006) The six domains of executive coaching. In H. Brunning (Ed.) *Executive Coaching: Systems-Psychodynamic Perspective*. London: Karnac.

De Haan, E. (2008) *Relational Coaching*. Chichester, UK: John Wiley & Sons.

Heron, J. (1975) *Helping the Client*. London: Sage.

Kets de Vries, M. F. (2006) *The Leader on the Couch*. Chichester, UK: John Wiley & Sons.

Maccoby, M. (2007) *Narcissistic Leaders: Who Succeeds and Who Fails*. Boston: Harvard Business School Press.

Peltier, B. (2010) *The Psychology of Executive Coaching*. East Sussex, UK: Routledge.

Further reading

Amado, G. (2009) Psychic imprisonment and its release within organisations and working relationships: OPUS Conference, London, 21–22 November 2008. *Organisational and Social Dynamics*, 9(1), 1–20.

Armstrong, D. (2005) *Organisation in the Mind*. London: Karnac.

De Haan, E. (2005) A new vintage: Old wine maturing in new bottles. *Training Journal*, November, 20–24.

De Haan, E. (2012) *Supervision in Action*. Maidenhead, UK: Open University Press, McGraw-Hill Education.

Hawkins, P. (2012) *Creating a Coaching Culture*. Maidenhead, UK: Open University Press, McGraw-Hill Education.

Hawkins, P. and Schwenk, G. (2006) *Coaching Supervision*. London: Chartered Institute of Personnel and Development.

Huffington, C. (Ed.) (2004) *Working Below the Surface*. London: Karnac.

Kets de Vries, M. F., Korotov, K. and Florent-Treacy, E. (Eds) (2007) *Coach and Couch*. New York: Palgrave.

Milan, M. and West, L. (2001) *The Reflecting Glass*. New York: Palgrave.

Obholzer, A. and Zagier Roberts, V. (Eds) (1994) *The Unconscious at Work*. London: Routledge.

Thornton, C. (2010) *Group and Team Coaching*. East Sussex, UK: Routledge.

Websites

British Association of Psychotherapists (BAP) http://www.bap-psychotherapy.org.

British Psychoanalytic Council (BPC) http://www.psychoanalytic-council.org.

UK Council for Psychotherapy (UKCP) http://www.psychotherapy.org.uk.

8

Application of presupposition in motivating change

Graham Megson

This chapter pays close attention to the language people use in their everyday exchanges and how it can affect perceptions of reality and, as a consequence, the change process.

The dictionary definition of a presupposition is anything assumed true beforehand as a basis of an argument. This relates to beliefs or assumptions that are not conscious, and are often embedded in the background within the basic structure of feelings, emotions and choice of verbal expression.

Leading change, whether it is for personal growth, development, or as part of a change management programme, requires a unique mix of influencing skills, persuasion techniques and coaching. It needs to take into account the individual and their reaction to change. Many models of change management have been developed over recent years, but one which blends the individual with the process is the change cycle.

The change cycle

We can look to some simple but accepted theory underpinning change. Many experts have written on this subject, most with very sound but differing 'rules' for getting it 'right'. However, we are all aware that each change is different, driven perhaps internally or externally, intentionally or foisted upon one. Therefore the more adaptive the leader, the more insightful and willing they are to explore options, the better most change projects will proceed.

A four-phase model of denial, resistance, exploration and commitment is a simple but seemingly effective indicator of reactions to change by individuals or groups (Figure 8.1).

Think hard about how each person, if they were standing on each part of the cycle, would be interpreting the behaviours of those who were standing on a different part of that continuum. Think about yourself, regarding a change you have experienced. Do you recognise the cycle in your processing of events? How did you feel about others who may have had polarised views to your own? What would a group in the denial 'camp' actually be saying (or internally saying to themselves) about those over there in commitment – who are busily trying to implement the initiative? What would the other three groups be saying about those in denial? It is not hard to see how conflict can arise. Nor is it hard to see the need to control this process.

The five stages of grief model of Elisabeth Kübler-Ross (1969; Table 8.1) might be worth exploring in the context of leading and being subject of change. The emotional roller-coaster, while perhaps not overt, will to some degree be in play. It will depend upon the profundity of the change and the starting presupposition of both the recipient and change agent/leader. It is worth remembering that often the change agent/leader has most likely had time to come to terms with the new position and will be in a 'different place' from the recipient.

Different people have different levels of reluctance or enthusiasm, or may need to know details and timelines.

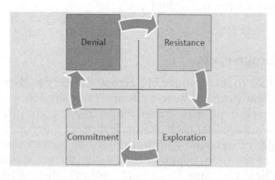

Figure 8.1 The change cycle

Table 8.1 **The five stages of grief**

Stage	Interpretation
1 Denial	Denial is a conscious or unconscious refusal to accept facts, information, reality etc. relating to the situation concerned. It is a defence mechanism and perfectly natural. Some people can become locked in this stage when dealing with a traumatic change that can be ignored. Death, of course, is not particularly easy to avoid or evade indefinitely.
2 Anger	Anger can manifest in different ways. People dealing with emotional upset can be angry with themselves and/or with others, especially those close to them. Knowing this helps in keeping detached and non-judgemental when experiencing the anger of someone who is very upset.
3 Bargaining	Traditionally, the bargaining stage for people facing death can involve attempting to bargain with whatever God the person believes in. People facing less serious trauma can bargain or seek to negotiate a compromise. For example, 'Can we still be friends?' when facing a break-up. Bargaining rarely provides a sustainable solution, especially if it is a matter of life or death.
4 Depression	Also referred to as preparatory grieving. In a way it is the dress rehearsal or the practice run for the aftermath, although this stage means different things depending on whom it involves. It is a sort of acceptance with emotional attachment. It is natural to feel sadness and regret, fear, uncertainty, etc. It shows that the person has at least begun to accept the reality.
5 Acceptance	Again, this stage definitely varies according to the person's situation, although broadly it is an indication that there is some emotional detachment and objectivity. People dying can enter this stage a long time before the people they leave behind, who must necessarily pass through their own individual stages of dealing with the grief.

Based on the grief cycle model of Elisabeth Kübler-Ross (1969). Interpretation by Alan Chapman (2006).

Some really do need to know the 'big picture' before they can work with the details – for others this is mere 'padding' and they want to work with smaller chunks of information. Therefore the role of leader in any change process is critical. Unfortunately, it is often the case that the people leading change do not see themselves as coaching or mentoring staff at the critical moments of transition and, as a result, change can be haphazard or slow (O'Connor and Lages, 2004). This chapter argues that the conscious use of language can help overcome, deflect or minimise resistance to change (Charvet, 1995).

I will focus on aspects of change and influence using the presuppositions drawn from neuro-linguistic programming (NLP), showing how they can be deployed using perceptual positions and logical levels (O'Connor and Seymour, 1990; Burn, 2005). Logical levels relate to our belief and value systems and our ability to transcend a current situation, to gain a different and more rounded perspective. In this context they can be seen as the backbone underlying the five stages of grief outlined by Kübler-Ross (1969).

When used in a conversational coaching style, these techniques can provide a powerful methodology for change and have proven enormously useful in a variety of business and development settings (Hall, 2001).

Our models of the world: what they say about us

Our presuppositions play a key role in setting the 'frame' or context and so are essential in overcoming resistance to change. The major controlling presuppositions of a given situation are rarely articulated. They get a free ride into the conversational background by virtue of the fact that their truth is required for any communication to make sense or have meaning in the given context.

A simple and well-used example is the phrase: 'the cat was sitting on the mat'. To properly attach a meaning to the sentence we have to assume the existence of objects and how they relate together. In this case there has to be a cat and a mat, and we understand that the cat did sit on the mat. A presupposition also has a property of being true when the sentence is negated: 'the cat was not sitting on the mat'. In this case the cat and the mat still exist, as does the relationship of one being able to sit on the other. In understanding the motivators that drive or block change it is necessary to appreciate how presuppositions support or defuse resistance by examining the relationships between the implied objects, beliefs and values.

At any given moment there are three major types of presupposition in play: *world, influencer,* and *client.* The world models not only our everyday process of living but also the finer context, such as an economic downturn, changes in financial imperatives or the appointment of a new chief executive. In management terms these may be seen as the maintenance or hygiene factors and, as such, fundamental to each individual.

The influencer and client presuppositions are a subset of the world presuppositions that make use of what Korzybski (2000), the founder of general semantics, termed the map–territory distinction. Korzybski famously said that 'the map is not the territory'. The intention being to draw a difference between what exists outside ourselves (the territory) and how we model what we experience by our senses to create internal representations (or maps) of that reality. Because we are embodied beings, all that we know is filtered by our senses and we draw correlations from our life experiences that create *deletions, distortions* and *generalisations* about the world.

Korzybski's dictum, the map is not the territory, is also cited as an underlying principle used in NLP, where it is used to signify that individual people do not in general have access to absolute knowledge of reality but in fact only have access to a set of beliefs they have built up over time, about reality. So it is considered important to be aware that people's beliefs about reality and their awareness of things (the map) are neither reality itself nor everything they could be aware of (the territory). The originators of NLP have been explicit that they owe this insight to general semantics.

Our correlations are subjective, hence the influencer (or change agent) and the client (or changee) may have significantly different models of a situation dictated by their unique life history up to the point of communication. A change to the world creates a ripple in the context, which may negate some or many of our presuppositions of the world at large. Csikszentmihalyi (2002), for example, suggests that we switch on the radio or TV news every morning largely to confirm that nothing fundamental has changed while we have been sleeping.

The myth of objectivity: cognitive dissonance

Change often fails because it is based on the false premise of objectivity. The reasoning is that if a person can just understand the logic or rationality of what is being proposed they will accept the changes. This is ill-informed on several counts. First, both the influencer and coachee have unique life experiences and so different maps of reality. The world is relative, not absolute. Second, because we are embodied beings everything we do is related to how we feel about given situations. Emotional discomfort is often associated with the discrepancy between what we already know (believe/value) and new information (or its interpretation). A name for this feeling is cognitive dissonance (Festinger, 1957).

The theory of cognitive dissonance is one of the most influential and extensively used theories in social psychology. The idea has withstood the test of time and repeated experimentation. What it tells us is that a certain threshold exists below which people will experience dissonance and adjust their inner organisation. Festinger called this the minimal justification hypothesis. The theory suggests that people have an inbuilt motivational driver that tries to reduce dissonance by changing their attitudes, beliefs or behaviours, or by justifying or rationalising them. Dissonance occurs when a person detects a logical inconsistency in their beliefs or values. Values and beliefs differ from facts precisely because they carry some emotional charge. This means that the dissonance is experienced as a state involving anger, sadness, fear, hurt, guilt, embarrassment and so forth, and is often strongest when we believe something about ourselves and do something or are forced to do something that contradicts that belief.

Dissonance increases with the importance of the subject to us, how strongly the states conflict, and our inability to rationalise (or explain away) the conflict. For example, believing that we are good and then doing something bad, being vegetarian and eating meat, or attending church regularly and then committing a sin. In fact, the internal projections that determine value judgements on our perceived morality, foolishness or gullibility are great sources of dissonance. Removing the tension associated with cognitive dissonance generally follows one or more of the following approaches:

- reducing the importance attached to the dissonant belief;
- changing the dissonant belief;
- adding congruent states until they outweigh the dissonant belief (rationalise).

Dissonance increases in proportion to the perceived importance and impact of making the decision. If the difficulty of reversing the decision is high enough then it becomes easier to change the internal relationship between our beliefs and values. However, if the dissonance becomes too great interesting side effects occur. Suppose someone is required to learn or accept something that contradicts what they already know. If they are particularly committed to this prior knowledge they are likely to resist the new learning. If something has been difficult, uncomfortable, humiliating or traumatic to learn, a person is less likely to accept that what they learnt was inappropriate or valueless. The latter means that the person would have to admit that they had been gullible or duped or had been wrong in some important way, which causes a strong emotional reaction.

Neighbour (1992) suggests that an important part of learning and change is the generation of sufficient dissonance to 'drive an intellectual wedge' between current beliefs and perceived reality. To overcome resistance requires that both influencer and client reconcile their different world view. Aronson (1973) concludes that it is not logical inconsistency that drives the resolution of dissonance but a psychological inconsistency. He argues that a human is not a rational animal but a rationalising animal that wants to appear reasonable to him or herself (Griffin, 2008, Chapter 16). Hence an essential part of managing change is in understanding how to manage or create dissonance. A useful starting point is to adopt a set of operating principles or presuppositions about how people behave in the world.

The NLP presuppositions: why we do what we do

Table 8.2 lists the core sets of presuppositions about people and their behaviour from NLP. These are all reasonable assumptions that try to separate *intention* from *behaviour*. The first two have been covered in the last section. Take a look at the rest and think about what things have to be true about people (including yourself) for the rest to have any meaning. Each statement, once you accept it, creates insight into how people are motivated and create dissonance for themselves in almost any situation.

Propositions P3–P5 express the view that if you enter a negotiation session with only one outcome and do not achieve it then you are at an impasse. Thus any change process must involve a number of ways to achieve the outcome, preferably including ones that can be embodied by the people required to make the change. A group that is too inflexible will get boxed into an evolutionary niche and be driven to extinction. In ecological systems it is known that a population must show the requisite variety for survival. This is particularly true in the context of major environmental shifts; for example, in governmental legislation and regulation, where the socio-political landscape or the market forces external to an organisation shift radically. A typical case in organisational terms is 'group-think'. The less flexible people or groups become the less able they are to survive major change. For the change specialist this means having a flexible approach in the use of language, presentation, style and content in order to 'roll with the punches' in a way that allows them to stay in control of the process and still achieve their objectives. This is particularly true in negotiations, where the person with the greatest number of fluid positions is most likely to achieve the outcome they want. It is necessary to create the *illusion* of choice.

Table 8.2 Fundamental presuppositions for leading change

Label	Presupposition	Interpretation
P1	The map is not the territory	You are always separated from reality. Dissonance occurs when things are 'not as they ought' to be.
P2	The mind and body are one system	We live our experience, which creates an experiential embodiment of any ideas or concept – including change.
P3	If you go on doing what you are doing now you will get the same results you are getting now	Everyone is responsible for their own lives; we can always control how we respond to events.
P4	If you want something to be different you must do something different	A variant of the principle of requisite variety for survival in complex systems. The most flexible person controls the system.
P5	The person with the greatest number of choices is likely to get the best outcome	Related to previous case and version of BATNA (best alternative to non-agreement) in negotiation.
P6	You cannot not communicate	Communication is either positively or negatively received. Doing nothing or avoiding responsibility is also a form of communication, which often has negative effects.
P7	The meaning of a communication is the response you get	People respond to what they think you mean, irrespective of what you think you mean or intend. People are incredibly sensitive to non-verbal language, which can negate any words you use if it is not congruent with them.
P8	Every behaviour has a positive intention	This does not mean that a person makes the best objective choice. People act in a way that is always positive (albeit unconsciously) for them.

Table 8.2 Continued

Label	Presupposition	Interpretation
P9	A person has all the resources they need	Everyone has the personal resources to deal with any situation. That is, they know deep down how the situation has occurred and what they need to do to make a change.
P10	Every behaviour is appropriate in some context	People adopt behaviours that have worked in the past. When the context changes they will need to find different behaviours.
P11	There is no such thing as failure, only feedback	When things turn out differently to what we expect we tend to see that as failure (which is a negative feeling). Alternatively, we have learned something about how not to do something (which is positive).

Communication: the meaning of rapport

Presuppositions P6–P7 describe how and why change leaders often get into trouble when selling something new. The principle behind *you cannot not communicate* is that we are embodied beings. Since ancient times we have communicated both consciously and unconsciously using verbal and non-verbal signals. What we say and the non-verbal signals we exude in any situation provide a rich source of information for anyone sensitive to read the signs. As a communicator of change it is imperative that our verbal and non-verbal messages are congruent.

Thousands of years of evolution, most of it before language emerged, means that people are unconsciously sensitive to these hidden signals. We cannot evade personal responsibility by saying nothing or being absent from key moments, because that communicates just as much as being present or making a verbal contribution. Likewise we cannot rely on purely verbal presentations to carry the message we want to deliver. The best way to summarise this is in the phrase: 'it's not what you say, it's how you say it.' Another well-used phrase is: 'walk the talk', which means being congruent with the message you are trying to sell.

Communications experts are fond of asking how responsible a person is for their communication. In a typical conversation, how much is someone responsible for the messages they are trying to convey? What do you think? In any form of communication we are absolutely 100 per cent responsible for our side of the message. A person will respond and react to what *they* think you have communicated. And, because we all have our own unique, subjective maps of the reality, this may or may not be an accurate translation of what you intended it to mean. A typical manager response to a difficult situation is to say: 'Well, I told them to change, so they should have changed.' A bunch of well-intentioned change seminars and PowerPoint presentations expounding the cold, logical, objective reality of why change is necessary leaves no scope for assessing and dealing with the response from the emotional interpretation. A summary of this from the client side is often: 'You're talking *at* me, not *to* me' or 'What you're saying just doesn't feel right.'

To be effective, a change leader needs to be constantly aware of how people are reacting to the message, and this requires rapport. Rapport for change purposes can be defined as the process of responsiveness at an unconscious level. It implies an ability to relate to others in a way that creates a climate of trust and understanding. Without rapport it is impossible to execute the magician's trick of creating change by first pacing the situation and then leading the client to the new situation. There are many books on body language, matching, mirroring and so forth. Neuroscientists have also indicated the existence of our predisposition for rapport through mirror neurons. Those aspects of rapport are important, but the greatest influence you can have is on matching presuppositions and translating your message into terms that people can understand in their own model of the world.

Two follow-on assumptions are that *there are no resistant clients, only inflexible communicators* and *resistance to change is a sign of a lack of rapport*. The first follows from P3–P4. Above all, a change leader should be a collector of different approaches to unlock the potential in any situation

– be prepared to *go the extra mile*, or *change tack if your approach isn't working*. The second makes most managers squirm. Quite often the very last thing they want is to get all 'touchy-feely' with a group of people who are making their life a misery. And, often, this is a reason for bringing in external consultants. This, however, misses the real meaning of rapport, which is to build trust so that people will follow you through the change. Since people tend to like and trust people who are like themselves this means discovering what lies at the core of an individual/group/organisation's maps of the world.

You may have heard the famous line about the definition of a management consultant as someone who borrows your watch and tells you what time it is. In truth, the change manager borrows your own neurological processes and uses them to create the requisite amount of dissonance in a way that will empower you to create the resources you need to change yourself.

At the heart of the process is the *illusion* of choice. The most flexible person will control the system and, as a change communicator, if you can lead the group/client to believe that they have made the changes themselves then resistance will melt away almost magically. This leads to the idea that the change manager is superfluous: 'I don't know what they do', 'We don't need them', 'I could do their job.'

Perceptual positions: finding points of resistance

Following Bateson (2000) and the logical levels of learning (Csikszentmihalyi, 2002), we can create some standard manoeuvres for change work:

- A confrontation between the presuppositions (model of the world) of the subject and communicator.
- Getting the person to act, in session or outside, in a way that confronts their own presuppositions.
- A demonstration that contradicts the premises controlling the subject's behaviour, or creation of some exaggeration or caricature of an experience enacting the old presuppositions.

In each case, the intention is to produce generative learning (or relearning) by the creation and resolution of dissonance. A simple way to create choice is to ask yourself or the group: 'What can we do differently?', 'What else can we be?', 'What would happen if . . .?', 'Suppose that we could . . .', 'How is that different . . . and how is it the same?' But a far more effective and indirect technique is the use of perceptual positions (Figure 8.2).

Perceptual positions is a technique that allows us to take multiple perspectives to produce greater influence on or insight to a given situation. The first position looks at the world from your own point of view: 'How does this affect me?, 'What am I thinking and feeling about this?' The second position considers the situation from another point of view: 'How does this appear to them?', 'How do they feel about this?' The third position is an objective (dispassionate) position of an independent observer: 'How would this look to someone not involved?' In some cases it is also useful to adopt a meta-position that looks at the whole grouping; for example, as an outside agency such as a parent company, government, regulatory or legislative body.

The technique can be used on many different levels with individuals, groups and with change leaders themselves. The latter being useful when they are a source of resistance for the client (e.g. a line manager). As a starting point the change facilitator should walk through the different positions, with themselves or a mentor, to identify their own personal preferences and limitations linking them back to the presuppositions in Table 8.2 to identify any potential limiting or

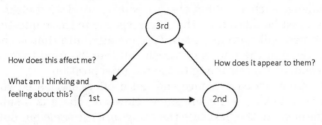

Figure 8.2 **Perceptual positions**

challenging beliefs that would affect their ability to facilitate the changes required. The change leader can then run the model with an individual or a group resistant to change. The context may vary, with the perspectives taking on different contexts such as relationships with individuals, different departments or organisational structures. The key though is to tease out the issues in relation to the presuppositions and identify the potential sources of dissonance or where the creation of dissonance would create movement.

The linguistic clues that we require for change can be summarised as *identifications, complex equivalence* and *cause–effect* (Bandler and Grinder, 1981; Dilts, 1999; Hall, 2001; Basu, 2009). These patterns are associated with phrases such as: 'I am . . .', 'X means Y', or 'X makes me Y'. These are distortion statements in that they take what is happening outside of ourselves and map it to our internal mental model of how we think the world is. Consequently, they tell us how someone models their world and how that empowers or limits them. When a person is asked to behave in a way that does not fit with their model of the world they become incongruent and the subsequent dissonance creates resistance.

Identifications are often nominalisations (process words that have become atrophied and fix the person in time); for example, I am a manager/teacher/salesman/nurse. In each case a process has been made static, so a person thinks they cannot be anything else. Suggesting that a manager joins the sales team, a teacher does research, a salesman becomes a regional manager or a nurse becomes a supervisor all require a shift that is not static. To overcome the resistance or inertia requires first denominalising the thing frozen using a challenge such as: 'What else are you? . . . And what else? . . . You must be more than that.' In response to these questions a person will normally identify some attribute that is characteristic of the new role, which can then be used to create movement via reframing to the required position.

Complex equivalence and cause–effect associate two or more things as being the same. However, there is a subtle difference. In the first case the things are the same but out of time (atemporal), indicating that they cannot be changed, whereas cause–effect indicates that things are the equivalent through time (temporal), implying that if one thing happens the other *must* happen as a consequence. Consequently, these patterns signal the type of reframing required and are often linked to an implicit feeling:

Reorganising the office that way means that I will be further away from the coffee machine/photocopier/ window and that makes me feel sad/angry/less valued.

Closing that division means there will be fewer managers and that makes me uncertain about my future/ worried about my job/angry that I'm being sidelined.

The words after 'makes' are often unspoken and may be a source of dissonance.

The implicit nature of the blockage makes reframing a complex and nuanced art. Thus, to overcome resistance it is necessary to understand the internal model a person holds and how that motivates their behaviour. The art of reframing is to break the associations or binds linking these concepts together. A simplification is to interpret each distortion statement as having a kind of polarity with the form: 'X *means/causes* Y, which *makes* me feel good/bad.'

A reframe then looks for a context in which a 'bad' feeling could be made into a 'good' feeling or to change the focus of attention in the current context to turn a bad feeling into a good feeling. If good/bad are too emotive then use positive/negative. Once the feeling shifts, resistance to change often disappears. For example:

Moving will give you more space and a bigger desk in a quieter part of the office. Surely you can see the advantages in that, can't you?

Yes, there will be fewer managers and that will create the resource for a team of expert troubleshooters who can be parachuted into problem areas at short notice. You're more than just a manager aren't you? What else could you be?

These various binds are discovered by listening to the exact words a person uses while you take them through the different perceptual positions. Presupposition P8 then allows the separation of intent from behaviour by finding what else the person gets out of the behaviour (a secondary gain) and providing an alternative way for the person to get it in the context of the change programme. In the examples, the person is questioning how valuable they are to the organisation and both answers indirectly reference how valued they are.

Conclusions

- Presuppositions are inherent barriers in managing in a change process. Resistance to change results from emotional dissonance, which can be understood and controlled by examining a small number of presuppositions (or assumptions) a person uses to make sense of the world.
- People should be helped to address and confront their own presuppositions.
- Akin to the grief cycle, managing/leading and coaching through change needs to take account of both the person's and coach/leader's presuppositions.
- Use of language and awareness of NLP provide powerful tools. Understanding how a person behaves linguistically helps to define how a person distorts, deletes or generalises important information about the world to create their own internal map. Listening acutely to how a person describes that map allows us to locate the source of dissonance and by choosing our words carefully allows us to influence by choosing words that change minds.
- Both verbal and non-verbal communications should be congruent, and the transmitter is responsible for both their intended message and that actually received or implied.
- Building rapport and trust is an essential part of the change process.
- Our own perceptions of the world are individually unique and fundamentally influence the starting position in any change process.
- People fundamentally avoid discord or dissonance with their values or beliefs.

- Flexibility and a number of strategies or outcomes (perceived or real) are more successful in assisting people through change.
- People tend to find it impossible to resist their own advice in the use of positive outcomes to promote positive perception and influence value and belief positions. Hence resistance can be attacked by empowering people to take control of the change itself. This can be achieved by understanding how a person organises their internal world.

References

Aronson, E. (1973) The rationalizing animal. *Psychology Today*, 23(3), 46–51.

Bandler, R. and Grinder, J. (1981) *Reframing: Neuro-Linguistic Programming and Transformation of Meaning*. Moab, UT: Real People Press.

Basu, R. (2009) *Persuasion Skills Black Book: Practical NLP Language Patterns for Getting the Response You Want*. Great Yarmouth, UK: Bookshaker.

Bateson, G. (2000) *Steps to an Ecology of Mind*. Chicago: University of Chicago Press.

Burn, G. (2005) *NLP Pocketbook*. Alresford, UK: Management Pocketbooks.

Chapman, A. (2006) *Elisabeth Kübler-Ross – Five Stages of Grief: Kübler-Ross Model for Death and Bereavement Counseling, Personal Change and Trauma*. Available at: http://www.business balls.com/elisabeth_kubler_ross_five_stages_of_grief.htm.

Charvet, S. R. (1995) *Words That Change Minds: Mastering the Language of Influence* (2nd ed.). Dubuque, IA: Kendall/Hunt Publishing.

Csikszentmihalyi, M. (2002) *Flow: The Classic Work on How to Achieve Happiness* (Revised ed.). London: Rider/Random House.

Dilts, R. (1999) *Sleight of Mouth: The Magic of Conversational Belief Change*. Capitola, CA: Meta Publications.

Festinger, L. (1957) *A Theory of Cognitive Dissonance*. Stanford, CA: Stanford University Press.

Griffin, E. (2008) *A First Look at Communication Theory*. New York: McGraw-Hill.

Hall, L. M. (2001) *Communication Magic: Exploring the Structure and Meaning of Language*. Carmarthen, UK: Crown House Publishing.

Korzybski, A. (2000) *Science and Sanity* (5th ed.; originally published 1933). New York: The Institute of General Semantics.

Kübler-Ross, E. (1969) *On Death and Dying*. Hove, UK: Routledge.

Neighbour, R. (1992) *The Inner Apprentice*. Plymouth, UK: Petroc Press.

O'Connor, J. and Lages, A. (2004) *Coaching With NLP*. London: Element.

O'Connor, J. and Seymour, J. (1990) *Introducing NLP: Psychology Skills for Understanding and Influencing People*. London: Mandala.

9

Action learning as a complement to the coaching ethos

Dawn Forman

What is action learning?

Action learning can take many different forms but essentially is learning which, by placing participants in a group of peers (an action learning set), leads to a change in the way the individual is thinking about a situation, thereby leading to a change in the action that is taken by that individual. Essentially, therefore, each individual brings a problem or issue he/she is dealing with, discusses this within a group in a confidential way and, through open questioning, is encouraged to think through the issue and the underlying assumptions, thereby driving a different way of moving forward from that which had hitherto been possible. This can be summarised as in Figure 9.1.

Action learning is used on many senior leadership and management programmes, including the Top Management Programme of the Leadership Foundation for Higher Education, where the process for action learning has been refined over the last 12 years and is clearly documented (Kennie, Middlehurst and Johns, 2004; Gentle, 2010).

While the format of questioning and the rules of engagement can differ within action learning sets, and differing models have been generated, research undertaken and refinement derived over the years, most people acknowledge that the originator of the concept of action learning was Reg Revans, who was a physicist at Cambridge University. Revans

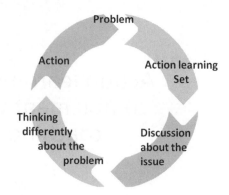

Figure 9.1 Action learning

(1998) found that, rather than speaking to other physicists about the problems or issues he was facing within his experimental work, if he could meet with a few other scientists and outline his issue, encourage his colleagues to ask him questions about the problem and questions about why this was a problem for him, he would start to think differently about the concern he originally had, and thereby move his thinking forward.

In addition, even when others brought their problems, by asking them questions it stimulated in his mind a reflection on whether the questions he was asking of the other persons were actually applicable to his own area. He was, therefore, again able to think differently about his original problem and found that the value of the action learning set and his time spent in these discussions far outweighed the time he would spend in working in isolation on the particular issue.

The view of Reg Revans has been replicated many times in many different forums. Managers who have had action learning sets created for them or have created them themselves often continue with these groups long after the need for the initial meeting or forum has passed. Indeed, many managers who move on to be leaders and CEOs of organisations still relate back to an action learning set they formulated when they were middle managers. CEOs who are still involved in action learning sets often indicate that the learning that takes place in these sets helps them to resolve issues that they may have been struggling to resolve for some time while working in isolation.

How does coaching fit into action learning?

Action learning can take many different forms, but if a peer coaching philosophy is used to underpin questioning of the individual it is seen to be more effective in helping the individual understand and find their own solution to the issue than when peers offer solutions to the problem posed. This is taking the view that the individual has all of the information available, is very much aware of the context and has often thought through the problem in greater detail than would be possible for any of the other individuals in the group. The individual posing the problem would also bring their own background to the issue and would need to take forward the problem and solution in their own way. Therefore it is not felt that giving the answer to the problem is appropriate, but allowing peers to coach the individual through the situation will help the individual far more to reflect, learn and take action forward in an appropriate way for themselves, the issue they are concerned with and the organisation as a whole.

How many people should be in the action learning set?

Generally, four to seven peers meet in the action learning set. Initially the group can meet as regularly as once every six weeks but, over time, the period between meetings may be extended to three to four months.

How do you set up an action learning set?

It is important that the group can bring a diversity of perspectives to the issues concerned. They are peers and therefore their level of experience is broadly similar. However, they may come from different organisations or departments within an organisation, and thereby have some understanding of the problems which may be raised but not an in-depth knowledge of the situation that the individual may be bringing.

If the group has not met previously, it is vitally important that in the initial session they gain an understanding of each other, disclosing their backgrounds and experience, and that they build a trust in the group. This is often facilitated by knowing that anything discussed in the group will not be discussed anywhere else within their organisations or even in their social lives. Once the group has been established, the trust should be such that the individuals can openly discuss the issues and personal concerns that they have without feeling threatened, undermined or in any way compromised.

How do you build that initial trust in the action learning set?

In order to ensure that a supportive, confidential and yet challenging environment can be developed between participants it is often helpful to encourage each participant to tell the group something about themselves personally. Generally, the more open participants can be, the better the bonding between participants and the better the action learning experience which will result.

A technique often used to great effect is outlined in *101 Coaching Strategies and Techniques* (McMahon and Archer, 2010). This is replicated here (Case Study 9.1) with permission from the editors.

Case Study 9.1   Understanding how previous life experiences have impacted on the client

This is a strategy that is used to deepen a client's understanding of how their previous life experiences impact on their behaviour today. The coaching assumption or belief is that deepening the client's self-awareness gives them a greater capacity to make fundamental shifts in their behaviour.

Clients can assess whether their behaviour patterns are still in service to them (i.e. are they still helpful?) or whether

---

certain behaviours result in difficulties for them. It is also a great way for clients to stand back and think about where they are going, either personally or in their careers. Typically, as a result of completing this exercise, clients find it easy to see where the 'pathway' is leading.

An influence that underpins this strategy comes from the work performed by life coaches. Life coaching can be focused: where the client is encouraged to set targets and a series of actions to help them reach their goals. The actions will be a step-by-step approach, leading towards their achieving their goals. This suggests that one can influence one's direction in life, rather than allowing events to dictate one's future. Here are the simple steps for building this self-awareness:

- *Step 1*   Using a flip chart or a wipe board, ask the client to draw a path or timeline from left to right and plot the most significant events throughout their life, leaving a section blank at the end of the path to represent their future.
- *Step 2*   Ask the client to talk each event through, asking why they chose that particular event, why it was significant to them and what the event/choice says about them. For example, if the client has highlighted a strong academic track record they may say that they have strength in analysis or creative writing, or that they enjoy research, or that they are driven to achieve a high standard of academic recognition. In focusing on these points the client will see more clearly what has motivated them.
- *Step 3*   Start with the earliest experiences, moving forward to the present day, and record comments the client makes. Once you have reviewed their pathway, look at the comments you have noted and ask the client to summarise their talents and typical behaviours.
- *Step 4*   Review the exercise and ask questions such as:
  - What are the main themes that have emerged for you?
  - What have you learnt about yourself?
  - What would others say about you?
  - How do these patterns of behaviour play out for you currently?
  - How do you believe that these patterns of behaviour will play out for you in the future?

How do the participants ensure they are ready to gain the most from the action learning experience?

Kets de Vries (2002, p. 60) provides a helpful list of preconditions for a willingness to learn and change through the action learning process. The outlines are:

- *Motivation* Is the member of the group ready to be challenged on some of his/her fundamental assumptions? Are they ready to relearn?
- *Capacity* Is each member of the group prepared to be open and honest?
- *Interpersonal skills* Can each participant quickly build a trusting and safe environment for all participants?
- *Emotional intelligence* Are they sufficiently aware of the emotions this type of work will invoke in themselves and equally sensitive to the emotions that may be invoked in others?
- *Psychological mindedness* Are potential participants open to learn more about themselves? Would they like to understand why they behave the way they do?
- *Capacity for introspection* Does each member of the group have the ability to reflect on experience and learn from links to the past?
- *Responses to observations of others* Are members of the group open to others seeking to provide a new perspective on the actions they have taken and unveil new interpretations of the attitudes of others?

Teasing out these preconditions for each member of the group will ensure an effective working relationship is established from the beginning and allow learning within the group to take place.

Are there any ground rules that need to be established for the group to work effectively?

The members of the action learning set are usually encouraged to derive their own ground rules. Common rules include:

- confidentiality;
- commitment to the group to be available when meetings are agreed;

- each person having the same amount of time allocated to deal with the issue they raise;
- a non-judgemental environment;
- a commitment to record action points and reflect on the learning that takes place.

Does each meeting follow a set format?

Again, the way in which action learning sets work varies but the following guidelines are helpful:

- It is advisable to have an experienced facilitator for the first four or five meetings. This person helps to establish the ground rules and the trusting environment. They will be familiar with the coaching technique of asking open questions and allowing the individual time to reflect.
- Each person should be allowed the same amount of time to discuss. The facilitator in the first instance usually keeps the time and the action points agreed by the individual, but after the first few meetings the participants can agree to do this for each other.
- Generally, in a 30-minute time frame for each individual, five minutes will be spent outlining the progress and the learning that has taken place since the previous meeting and stating the issue or area the individual would like to discuss on this occasion. Five minutes will then be spent with the group clarifying the issue and thereby agreeing an informal contract for the individual. Fifteen minutes will be spent in 'coaching' or asking open questions and five minutes will be spent agreeing the actions and noting any learning that has taken place during the session.

How does learning lead to action?

It is important that the action learning set is seen as much more than an opportunity to moan about the situation that the individual may be bringing. Learning and development is about the ability to get something done and not about the ability to talk about getting something done. Action learning should therefore facilitate diagnosis, analysis, experimentation, action and implementation (Figure 9.2).

Figure 9.2 **What action learning should facilitate**

Can you give any examples of the types of open questions that could be used?

The sort of open questions used can be dependent on the issue being raised, but a few very general questions often help the individual to question their actions and reflect more deeply:

- How do you feel about the situation?
- What do you want? What else?
- What is most important to you in this situation?
- What could you do differently?
- What assumptions are you making about the situation?
- What do you need to do first?
- What could be the cost to you of not solving this problem?
- Why do you believe what you want is reasonable?
- What about this situation causes you most anxiety or distress?
- What is positive about the situation?
- What is the simplest thing you could do?
- What will happen if you are not successful in getting what you want?
- How does this situation affect you personally?
- If you get what you want, what will this achieve for you?

How do you prompt the learning experience?

The learning experience will be derived by encouraging the individual to reflect. People learn in different ways, but some of the following questions may prompt the learning experience:

- How do you feel about the situation now?
- What would you do differently next time?
- Has this experience told you anything about yourself, your assumptions, your values, your prejudices?
- What would have made this better?
- What are you most proud of?
- What do you remember thinking but not saying?
- What should you definitely not have done?
- What surprised you about the situation?

Should you review how the action learning set is working?

It can be helpful from time to time to review whether everyone is still getting the same value out of the action learning set. The following questions can be helpful in such a review:

- Are we still following the same ground rules or do these need to be revised?
- What have I learnt over the past few action learning sets that I now need to consolidate if I am going to improve my way of working and learning?
- Do I still view this group as a group of peers who can add value to my thinking, or have they or I moved on?
- Is someone in the group irritating me and how am I going to deal with that situation?

How can you ensure you close the action learning set appropriately?

An action learning set that has lasted more than six meetings will undoubtedly have left a lasting impression on each of the participants. It is important therefore, when agreeing to close the action learning set and for each of the participants to go their separate ways, to close the group in an appropriate way. The following questions may help with this process:

- What impact have the action learning sessions had on my learning?
- What (if anything) has been a surprise?
- If I were to form another action learning set, what would I want to be clear about?
- What do I need to do now as a result of what I have learnt?
- What have I valued most about each of the individuals in the action learning set?

In addressing the last question it is often helpful for each person to indicate in turn their honest and open appreciation of each of the members and to own and celebrate the success of the group.

Conclusion

Although we live in an age where forming another group and agreeing to another set of meetings could justifiably be frowned upon, action learning sets are an easy route into starting a coaching philosophy in the work environment. They have been shown to be very effective both in aiding problem solving and in encouraging reflection in learning by the individuals involved. Following the guidance set out in this chapter should ensure the action learning set philosophy is appropriately and effectively established within, and indeed outside, the working environment.

References

Gentle, P. (2010) The influence of an action learning set of affective and organizational culture factors. *Action Learning Research and Practice*, 7(1), 17–28.

Kennie, T., Middlehurst, R. and Johns, A. (2004) *The Action Learning Tool Kit*. London: The Leadership Foundation for Higher Education.

Kets de Vries, M. F. R. (2002) *Can CEOs Change?: Yes But Only If They Want To*. Fontainebleau, France: INSEAD Working Paper 2002/36/ENT.

McMahon, G. and Archer, A. (Eds) (2010) *101 Coaching Strategies and Techniques*. Hove, UK: Routledge.

Revans, R. (1998) *ABC of Action Learning*. London: Lemos and Crane.

Further reading

Cooperrider, D. L. and Whitney, D. (1999) *Collaborating for Change: Appreciative Inquiry*. San Francisco, CA: Barrett-Koehler Communications.

McGill, I. and Beaty, L. (2001) *Action Learning*. London: Kogan Page.

Pedler, M. (2008) *Action Learning for Managers*. Aldershot, UK: Gower.

Revans, R. (1971) *Developing Effective Managers*. New York: Praeger.

Revans, R (1980) *Action Learning New Approaches for Managers*. London: Blond and Briggs.

Revans, R. (1982) *The Origins and Growth of Action Learning*. Bromley, UK: Chartwell-Bratt.

Weinstein, K. (1999) *Action Learning: A Journey in Discovery and Development*. Aldershot, UK: Gower.

10

Simple techniques to get you started

Dawn Forman

In a recent survey undertaken by the Institute of Leadership and Management (2011), organisations responded that 80 per cent of them had used coaching in some way over the last five years. Many indicated that in the difficult times we are living in today the potential for managers to coach their staff from poor to good, or from good to great is huge. Many organisations start the process with their top management team being coached. Managers gain skills in coaching and use its approach on a regular basis as part of their ongoing conversations with the people they line-manage; they have the benefit of being on hand to have brief coaching conversations as well as more formal sessions, which can be built in to the calendar.

Selecting external coaches for the organisation's top management team and looking at the criteria for assessing an external coach are dealt with in Chapter 12. This chapter, therefore, will provide some guidelines and help for starting to manage the coaching of individual staff and teams.

Agreeing the contract

In any coaching discussion, however brief, it is best to clarify what the coachee expects to gain from the coaching conversation. In a sense this is agreeing a contract, which both parties can review as the discussion goes forward. Hargaden and Sills (2002) outline the various types of contract, as set out in Figure 10.1.

Type of contract

'Hard', verifiable, sensory-based

Clarifying 'The main thing is to let the main thing be the main thing'	**Behavioural outcome** 'I know what I want to change' Client statement
Exploratory 'Till we have faces'	**Growth and discovery** 'I want more of myself' Client statement

No self-understanding

Self-understanding

'Soft', subjective, emergent

Figure 10.1 The coaching contract – a mutual commitment (Hargaden and Sills, 2002)

The coaching conversation can be for: clarifying the main purpose; bringing about changes in behaviour (this may be from the perspective of the coach or manager or it may indeed be that of the client); fostering growth and discovery (e.g. career development, dealing with a challenging situation); or can be exploratory (e.g. testing out proposals).

Taking notes for the session

Once the contract has been agreed, it is always helpful to have some form of notes taken of the session. It should be agreed what the format of these notes should be and clear that they are for the guidance of the individual and the person undertaking the coaching session. They are not to be disclosed to a third party. To help the confidentiality of this process, it is helpful to use the initials of the individual rather than the full name. A note should be made of the date or the number of the session being undertaken.

A statement of what the contract is that has been agreed should be included. If possible, there should be a note of what the coachee hopes to get out of the session. At the end of the session the same notes can be used to jot down the learning points that have been achieved, what reflections have been covered, the actions to be undertaken prior to the next session, any feelings expressed by the coachee and any observations made by the coach in terms of body language or feelings that they have had during the session.

It should be clear at all times that coaching is different from mentoring and counselling and, if necessary, the coach may advise the client or individual to progress towards counselling, should this be necessary. This is covered in Chapter 7.

Encouraging reflection and coaching questions

When a manager is undertaking coaching within the organisation it is all too easy for him/her to assume that he/she knows the answers to the question being posed or the topic or issue being discussed by the coachee. To avoid providing the answer when undertaking a coaching session, the two simple techniques of encouraging reflection and coaching questions are often helpful.

Encouraging reflection

The coach should be encouraging the coachee to reflect at all times. Using the word REFLECT as an acronym is often useful for the coach:

R is for reminding the coach to develop the Relationship: building the relationship of trust will enable the coachee to be more open and expressive.

E is for Engaging: engaging the client in productive conversations.

F is for Feeling: encouraging the individual to express how they are actually feeling about the event and, indeed, for any feelings that the discussion brings about in the coach him/herself.

L is for Listening: listening attentively to what the individual is saying and ensuring they understand – if they have listened effectively and can repeat back to the individual what they have said in a summary. This often helps to move the coachee into a different level of consideration.

E is for Exploring: exploring what the client actually means and what options and activities could be undertaken in a coaching scenario to encourage the client to deal with the situation.

C is for Challenge: is the individual actually interpreting the situation appropriately or are they making assumptions; a common error which can be made by the person being coached. Challenging the individual can also help them to develop, but it must be remembered that the challenging conversation must be done in a safe environment.

T is for Timely: coaching interventions should be made in a timely manner. This is where a coaching philosophy within an organisation is very helpful, as coaching discussions can take place on the spot rather than waiting for a more formal event to take place.

Coaching questions

For people who are new to coaching it is often helpful for them to be reminded to ask questions that start with 'What . . .?', 'Who . . .?', 'Where . . .?', 'How . . .?', 'If . . .?', 'Imagine . . .', 'So . . .' (as in 'So, what does this mean for you?'). Colombia University, in its organisational consultancy programme, offers the following questions as a stimulus for coaches to gain supplementary information:

- What is the issue for you in this?
- What makes it an issue now?
- How important is it for you on a 1–10 scale?
- How much energy do you have for finding a solution?
- What have you tried already?
- Imagine the problem has been solved; what would you see, hear, experience differently?
- What is standing in the way of the outcome you'd like?
- What responsibility can you take for changing things?
- What signs are there that things might be improving or be better than you imagine?
- Imagine you are at your most resourceful and resilient; what do you say to yourself about this issue?
- If you had all the courage and insight you needed, what would you do? What are your options for action here?

- What criteria do you have for judging those options?
- Against your criteria, what seems the best?
- So what is the next step?
- What action will you take?

Is your business ready?

In the changing environment in which we live, it is clear that coaching can aid staff adapting to change – empowering them to be flexible and align their agendas with those of the organisation. It is key, however, before embedding coaching within an organisation, for managers to ask some key questions of themselves:

- Are my personal and business goals in alignment to avoid conflict between my personal aspirations/values and business decisions?
- Do I appreciate the business?
- Am I professionalising management flowing from a focused leadership?
- Am I resourced and funded for growth?
- Am I managing transition to future ownership?

If a positive response can be gained to these questions, the manager can be more confident about taking the next stage.

The amygdala effect

It is important to remember that coaching is underpinned by psychological theory and practice. Its basis is that the individual has the necessary knowledge and ability to be able to make the changes. Even when the manager is the coach, they cannot possibly know all the intricacies of the relationships that an individual is experiencing or their interpretation of events and, indeed, if a manager presumes to know the answers, the individual will not grow and innovation will be stifled.

Coaching therefore does not deal in depth with historical matter. However, the manager as a coach should be conscious of what is called the amygdala effect – whereby the brain will automatically make a response if it believes a similar situation has been experienced previously. For example, a person who is giving up sugar in their coffee may, if they lose concentration, go to put sugar in their coffee even when they know this no longer applies. This unconscious reflex action can occur in a relationship situation, particularly at work. An individual may feel that they have come across a situation or relationship previously, and react in a similar way. They may relate it to a home situation or to one that has previously occurred at work. In a coaching session therefore it may be helpful to ask if a similar situation has arisen previously and if the coachee has reacted to the situation in a similar way. Raising the coachee's awareness of their reactions may help them to change the way they react in the future. An example is given in Case Study 10.1.

Case Study 10.1   Raising the coachee's awareness

Joan was a very busy and productive person at work. She was admired because she had always managed to complete a task effectively and efficiently. However, she had recently been promoted to undertake more of a project management role. This had meant more planning was necessary, more involvement with other members of the team, and it was necessary to ensure that everyone was on board with the time scales and that all aspects of the project had been thought through. Joan had undertaken some considerable background work. She was really keen to ensure that this project went well.

Key to the implementation of this project, however, was working with Joe and, from her previous experience of working with Joe she knew him to be slow and to over-complicate proceedings. In the midst of a very busy day implementing the project, Joan wanted to see him to outline that there was an issue with a particular piece of equipment. Joe was soon dismissive of the issues that were raised and, as a new piece of equipment had been purchased, Joan indicated that Joe should ask the supplier for a replacement.

Obtaining the replacement caused a further delay and when the new piece of equipment arrived this did not work either.

Joan therefore became all the more frustrated with Joe that this issue had not been resolved quickly.

Perhaps because the example Joan had given related to a piece of equipment, Joan quickly thought of what she had undertaken at the weekend. She had travelled some distance to visit her mother. The fridge-freezer in her mother's house had previously been making a funny noise. When she had found that it was now not working she assumed the freezer had broken. She had therefore immediately gone to order a new one. When she came back and went to put the oven on she found that this too did not work. She remembered that her sister had said that her mother had had fish and chips a lot from the local shop during the previous week. Joan therefore also assumed that the cooker had somehow mysteriously broken down. Joan was getting increasingly frustrated, as she seemed to be the only one who was making sure that things worked appropriately. She decided she needed to calm down a little and have a cup of tea.

She went to put the kettle on and suddenly realised that the kettle was no longer working either. It was therefore apparent that perhaps it was not any of the individual pieces of equipment but may be a fuse that needed to be replaced.

Coaching methods

As a manager becomes more experienced in coaching they can then go on to choose an appropriate method for the coaching situation that the coachee is outlining. De Haan and Burger (2004) summarise seven methods, a brief outline of which is given in Table 10.1.

Conclusion

Simple techniques can introduce coaching quickly and effectively into an organisation, thereby enabling it to achieve the benefits outlined in *Creating a Coaching Culture* (Institute of Leadership and Management, 2011), which states: 'Coaching needs to be supported at the very top of the organisation, but not limited to senior executives.'

Table 10.1 Coaching methods

	When can it be used?	Recommended where there is/are	Not recommended where there is/are
GROW method	Broadly applicable, even to short, specific issues	High motivation but little idea of possible ways to move forward	Emotional issues, non-specific issues, double meanings
Ironic method	Broadly applicable	Coachees who do not take responsibility and instead ask the coach for advice	Low self-confidence, lack of confidence in coaching
Paradoxical method	In the case of ambiguous, internally contradictory questions to the coach	Strongly ambiguous messages and unclear motivation for coaching	No strong and absolutely necessary reasons for using it
Solution-focused method	Broadly applicable, especially to practical issues	Discouragement, anxiety about the future	Coaches not prepared to consider their own share in the problem
Counselling method	Broadly applicable, especially in a longer-term coaching relationship	Lack of self-confidence or self-motivation	Need for a critical sparring partner
Analytic method	Broadly applicable, especially to multi-layered and emotional problems	Coaches not prepared to consider their own share in the problem	Need to achieve quick results and find solutions, low self-confidence
Ladder method	Multi-layered problems, including short, specific issues	Willingness and ability to consider the coachee's own assumptions	Non-specific issues, highly emotional issues

De Haan and Burger (2004).

References

De Haan, E. and Burger, Y. (2004) *Coaching with Colleagues: An Action Guide for One-to-One Learning*. Basingstoke, UK: Palgrave Macmillan.

Hargaden, H. and Sills, C. (2002) *Transactional Analysis: A Relational Perspective*. Hove, UK: Brunner-Routledge.

Institute of Leadership and Management (2011) *Creating a Coaching Culture*. London: ILM. Available at: https://www.i-l-m.com/downloads/publications/G443_ILM_COACH_REP.pdf.

Further reading

De Haan, E. (2008) *Relational Coaching: Journeys Towards Mastering One-to-One Learning*. Chichester, UK: Wiley.

Watzlawick, P., Weakland, J. and Fisch, R. (2011) *Change: Principles of Problem Formation and Problem Resolution*. New York: W. W. Norton.

11

Measuring the success of your organisation's achievements through coaching

Gwen Wileman

When you create a culture of coaching, the result may not be directly measurable in dollars. But we have yet to find a company that cannot benefit from more candour, less denial, richer communication, conscious development of talent, and disciplined leaders who show compassion for their people.

(Sherman and Freas, 2004)

Coaching in organisations is on the increase: how do we know it works?

It appears that only one-third of organisations actually undertake any assessment of the tangible benefits of coaching and its impact on the organisation. It appears that formal evaluation of coaching initiatives is often lacking, with a great deal of reliance on anecdotal evidence to measure effectiveness.

This chapter seeks to explore alternative approaches to measuring the impact of coaching on an organisation, and to understand why and to what extent this matters and how effective various evaluation approaches actually are.

Coaching takes place in eight in ten (82 per cent) organisations. Among those in which it does take place, only one-third (36 per cent) have a system to evaluate it. Systems rely mainly on the collection of post-course evaluations (58 per cent), individuals' testimonies (56 per cent), assessing the impact on business key performance indicators (KPIs) (44 per cent), and measuring the return on expectation (40 per cent) (Chartered Institute of Personnel and Development [CIPD], 2010).

Assessment of the tangible benefits of coaching is important. There should be accountability on the part of the coach, closure for the individual and data to prove the value of coaching for the organisation. The lack of systematic evaluation of coaching is seen as a huge gap in demonstrating its effectiveness; however, for others the value of coaching is seen in the day-to-day changes in transformational behaviour of individuals.

The measurement process

There are three different levels of evaluation of coaching (Carter and Peterson, 2006):

1 *Effectiveness*   Did the coaching work?
2 *Impact on individuals*   What did the person do as a result of being coached?
3 *Organisational and business results*   What was the value of the coaching to the organisation?

Carter and Peterson recommend a five-step evaluation process for measuring organisational coaching programmes: preparation, design, implementation, analysis and communication of findings.

The case studies included in this chapter highlight some of the challenges behind what in essence seems a very simple process. There are some important steps to take which can enhance the likelihood of the evaluation process going smoothly and providing reliable data. The first is to plan how to evaluate before the coaching programme starts. Also, keep the process simple and focus on a few key indicators, but do not rely on a single measure. It is important to tell people up front it is happening to ensure their cooperation in the feedback process.

Measuring progress towards a coaching culture

Clutterbuck and Megginson (2005) believe that coaching has the potential to set the tone for the way relationships are managed throughout an organisation; in their words, the 'coaching way'. They have developed a model and a set of tools, which can be used selectively, to measure the move to a coaching culture in individual organisations. This is an important reference for any organisation embarking on a project to begin to measure the impact of coaching in their organisation. There is not sufficient space in this chapter to focus on this one model in detail; however, there are many indicators that coaching is more successful when the culture is supportive. Establishing where your organisation sits on the nascent, tactical, strategic or embedded continuum outlined by Clutterbuck and Megginson will help you develop an agenda for action to support your coaching investment and maximise its impact.

The concept of a coaching scorecard

An alternative approach is the coaching scorecard (Leedham, 2005). This is a holistic approach to evaluating the benefits of business coaching and is an adaptation of the 'SMART performance pyramid' (Cross and Lynch, 1988). Leedham believes this 'coaching benefits pyramid' model provides a valid and holistic picture of the effectiveness of a business coaching relationship from the perspective of and for the benefit of all stakeholders.

The model is based on the principle that to be fully effective a business coaching relationship needs to be built on the firm foundation of four key factors. These are the skills of the coach, the personal attributes of the coach, the coaching process and the coaching environment. If these foundation factors are in place the 'inner' personal benefits of clarity and focus, confidence and motivation can be realised by the coachee. This then moves to the important stage – what did the individual actually do as a result of being coached? As a result of realising the inner personal benefits they display (for all to see) enhanced skills, knowledge and understanding and improved behaviours. Finally, with these enhanced skills and behaviours the individual will be equipped and empowered to achieve business results in the form of improvements in performance, increased productivity or better problem solving (Figure 11.1).

This is a relatively sophisticated model, which can be used to measure whether a coaching contract has delivered benefits, but can require data collection and analysis not easily available in all organisations.

Options for measuring the impact

Evaluation can thus be based on a number of different approaches. It is true, however, as with other HR activities, that measuring the return on investment in coaching is difficult because it is hard to isolate the impact of the coaching intervention on organisational performance indicators such as financial performance or customer satisfaction. To do nothing, however, may lead to the conclusion that coaching is not valuable, has little impact and is therefore not worth investing in – a 'nice to do' as opposed to a powerful intervention with impact on people and business performance.

At the transformational level the cultural change can be crucial, but not immediately visible.

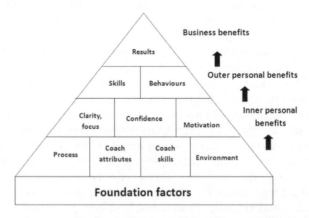

Figure 11.1 Coaching benefits pyramid (Leedham, 2005; adapted from Cross and Lynch, 1988)

There are therefore two ends of the spectrum. At one end is the view that hard measures of return on investment must be in place to justify coaching – despite the difficulties of isolating impact and the time and effort needed to gather evidence. The other end of the spectrum is to simply 'believe in the process', gather anecdotal evidence at the individual level and trust that this will impact on organisational performance!

Clearly neither is likely to be either effective or appropriate for specific organisations, and so a framework for evaluation needs to be designed which is specific to the organisation. The willingness to ensure adequate planning and resources are made available is critical. Through discussion, the outcome and approach will depend on the type of organisation, the maturity of the coaching culture and the 'buy-in' from senior executives. It will also change over time.

When embarking on coaching in your organisation, think carefully about the objectives driving the initiative and therefore the most appropriate approach to assessing the organisational impact of the coaching intervention. Some options include the performance of the coach, improved performance ratings of the coachee, improved retention, achievement of coaching objectives, and comparison of pre- and post-coaching 360-degree feedback ratings.

Feedback from the sponsor (often HR), the individual, the line manager and top management are all important when assessing the effectiveness of a coaching intervention. It is essential, however, to consider the higher-level criteria in line with Kirkpatrick's four-tier model of evaluation (Kirkpatrick, 1994).

In summary, when selecting options for evaluation it would be useful to look at criteria to determine the impact on the individual, the degree of behavioural change and the degree of improvement in business effectiveness, and select those for which data are available or can be obtained within reasonable limits identified by the organisation.

Preparation: evaluation up front

When considering coaching interventions, seven in ten organisations either frequently or occasionally discuss the organisation's expectations of coaching with the line managers and coaches (71 per cent), and assess the likelihood that individuals/teams will benefit from coaching before embarking on it (69 per cent). More than half (55 per cent) specify the outcomes at the outset linked to the performance and appraisal system, while only two in five (40 per cent) contract with the parties involved to ensure data are collected for evaluation (CIPD, 2010).

In planning for evaluating coaching impact before the coaching assignment begins, it is important to think through how you intend to evaluate it (Carter and Peterson, 2006). The sponsor (usually HR) should work with the line manager and the coach at an early stage to establish realistic ways of monitoring progress and success. This will include clarifying the purpose of the evaluation, the audience for the results, resource availability and any obstacles to achieving reliable data and feedback.

In many coaching relationships this planning phase will start with a three-way meeting between the coach, line manager and individual to discuss how the coaching intervention will work. Issues that need to be discussed up front include confidentiality, the reporting of information, the structure of coaching sessions and how the manager and HR (if involved) will receive information about the effectiveness of the coaching.

This meeting is often referred to as three-way contracting, and although it is not always easy to agree the terms up front, this can be achieved with determination and skill. Once established, the smooth running of the contract and the ongoing relationship is more assured as it is based on relevant and measurable positive impact on both the individuals and the organisation. It is a vital part of demonstrating the impact and value of a coaching intervention to an organisation. This early planning phase is extremely important and has enabled some real achievements to be demonstrated through measurement rather than simply anecdotes.

Coaches apply varying levels of commitment to this sometimes difficult activity of three-way contracting. Claire Pedrick, an experienced coach and the Managing Director of 3D Coaching, I believe demonstrates some particularly good practice in this aspect of the coaching process. Case Study 11.1, based on the 3D experience, offers some useful 'how to' tips and the important factors to consider during contracting.

Case Study 11.1   Three-way contracting: Learning from the 3D experience

The ability to reflect on both the positives and the opportunities for improvement from each coaching assignment is critical. Some of these contracting issues can be difficult to resolve in the early stages of a coaching relationship with an organisation. The urgency, for example the need for an external fix for a thorny problem, can mean it is tempting to be less than thorough at the contracting stage. This may lead to relationship difficulties over time and between the parties and can make the impact extremely difficult to measure.

How to do it
- Push the sponsor to be very specific and with transformational outcomes – not just tasks; try to clarify the real changes that will be achieved in the person receiving coaching.
- Document this, in a simple written agreement, and ensure everyone signs up.
- Agree how additional issues that emerge during the coaching sessions are going to be dealt with. In the main it will be appropriate to explore these with the person, but it needs to be in an organisational context.
- Understand very clearly the balance between what is confidential in the room and what comes back to the sponsor (or to the client).
- Ensure any work done with individuals is in an organisational context to ensure the return on investment for the organisation is maximised.
- All parties must buy in to the agreed approach, otherwise the contract can be difficult to manage and the measurement becomes impossible, or at best unreliable.
- It is important to explore:

- What is a good outcome for you. (May be developed in
  1:1 coach and individual conversation first)
- What is a good outcome for the team.
- What is a good outcome for the organisation.

Why this is important

When a coaching assignment is transformational rather than transactional the contracting conversation can be much more difficult to conduct, especially when the required change is significant and far reaching for both the individual and the organisation. There are four key factors to consider:

1 *Independence*   Ensure that three-way contracting maintains the independence of the individual and that the coach does not end up as a conduit for 'he says/she says'.

2 Example 1:   An individual was having real difficulty with how they were being managed by their immediate manager and they needed to go and talk to the manager about this. However, the three-way contract was unclear and because of this it was easy for the coach to go back and tell the manager what should really have been said by the coachee. It looked like the coach was criticising the manager and the individual coachee did not take appropriate responsibility.

3 *Clear behavioural outcomes*   Establish clarity about what behavioural changes need to happen. Only then will transformation that will fully impact the organisation be likely to occur.

4 Example 2:   An organisation was aware that it had a staff member whose performance was unsatisfactory. A coach was asked to work with the individual around performance but there was no clarity around what an improvement would look like. The organisation did not get the outcomes it wanted. The coach was unfortunately sucked into the individual's problem.

5 *Incomplete agreement*   The sponsor, individual and coach must all buy in to the three-way contract and be clear about outcomes and behaviours.

6 Example 3:   An organisation invested in coaching for senior staff. This was tentatively agreed verbally and the coaching

went ahead. One person never signed off the verbal agreement in writing and the organisation was unable to hold them to account when they stopped being willing to engage in the coaching intervention. This impacted negatively on the value of the coaching investment to the organisation.

7 *Meta-contract*   When a number of coaches are going to work with a team of people, individual three-way contracts are important for each coaching relationship. However, this intervention could be much more transformational if it were seen as 'coaching the system in the organisation'. That will only happen if there is an overriding meta-contract in place, which helps where coaching interventions need to be integrated.

8 Example 4:   An organisation invited a team of coaches from 3D to work with their top team. All the three-way contracts were watertight. It became clear, without any breach of confidentiality, that there were thematic and interpersonal issues going on and that the organisation would benefit from some members of the team receiving coaching together. A meta-contract would have provided a framework and permission for a valuable conversation to have happened much earlier.

This case study highlights the importance of planning and contracting in setting and managing expectations as well as providing the basis for evaluation.

Some specific measures of effectiveness

Case Study 11.2 demonstrates how data, both qualitative and quantitative, can be used to measure the effectiveness of coaching in a university. A combination of a 'light touch' audit to measure how comfortable and confident individuals felt about implementing a new performance review process, alongside a selection of questions from the three-yearly staff survey, provide a comprehensive framework of assessment with minimum additional cost.

Case Study 11.2   Using staff surveys to measure effectiveness

De Montfort University (DMU) is a successful university seeking to ensure its distinctiveness and success in a very challenging and rapidly changing higher education environment. At the outset, the introduction of coaching into the organisation could be described as emergent (see Chapter 6).

In 2006, as a result of relatively poor staff survey scores around appraisal and development, a priority area for action within the HR strategy was to improve the process, skills and buy-in of the performance and development review process (PDR). Changing the perception of the PDR from a chore to a really worthwhile experience for both the manager and employee, given the history and the cynicism with which performance reviews were seen, was a significant challenge!

An agreement was reached with trade unions. Buy-in from managers, employees and trade unions was secured not only as a result of a simplified process but also by a name change that put a more positive spin on the whole approach. It became the achievement and development review (ADR).

The next step was to prepare managers and staff for the introduction of the ADR through a coaching approach. This was achieved through a major programme of blended learning to support the introduction of the ADR, which was grounded in the use of coaching skills and the belief that line manager as coach would be a very positive and successful way of encouraging higher levels of performance and significantly higher motivation. The approach was further integrated by the development of coaching skills and executive coaching for participants as part of the university's senior leadership development programme.

Coaching is reflected in a number of dimensions within the staff survey measurement framework. The success of a coaching approach to ADR is evidenced in Tables 11.1 and 11.2.

Line manager feedback

The shift of responsibility [for the ADR] from the reviewer to the reviewee helps develop empowerment.

Table 11.1 **Staff survey results**

Questions	2006 (%)	2010 (%)
Motivation	69	89
Achievement	81	93
University commitment to training and development	76	92
ADR is constructive	56	81

ADR, achievement and development review.

Table 11.2 **ADR 'light-touch' audit**

Questions	2006 (%)	2010 (%)
Completion rate	No data exist	92
I felt prepared for my ADR	No data exist	85
Preparing the form in advance was beneficial	No data exist	93
I was satisfied with my review meeting	No data exist	89

ADR, achievement and development review.

It makes more sense for me to support my staff's development rather than take the prime responsibility for making it happen.

Appraisee feedback

I felt that the ADR process was a vast improvement on the PDR in terms of shifting the responsibility and the thought process onto the reviewee. It gave a lot more opportunity to go into greater depth with the reviewer and identify goals and a clear work schedule for the year ahead.

Good opportunity for thinking, planning and reflecting. A useful contribution to personal and work development. Good vehicle for staff development and recognition of achievement, and for identification of potentially difficult or unsatisfactory issues.

The term 'coaching' is being used much more in a positive context than when coaching was emergent. Coaching features in a significant number of ADR development plans as a planned development intervention.

There is significant evidence that sophistication in coaching requests is developing – by genre, for example career coaching, performance coaching and leadership coaching, and by theme, for example change management, handling difficult conversations and conflict resolution.

The impact of using a coaching approach to support the new ADR process has not only improved the ADR process, but has further developed the ongoing coaching culture where 'the coaching way' is becoming a preferred way of managing and leading at DMU.

(Vincent Cornelius, Learning and Development Advisor, De Montfort University, 2011)

The positive data in this case study indicate very strongly that ADR through coaching has been widely successful, and a much greater impact than was originally anticipated has been achieved. The communication of these data will in itself reinforce and enhance the coaching culture.

Conclusions

- In the context of coaching, the research suggests that that there should be much more focus on appropriate measurement and evaluation. The extent and depth of this, however, needs to be organisation specific.
- Feedback from HR, the individual, the line manager and senior management are all valuable when assessing the effectiveness of the coaching intervention. Ideally, criteria should include evidence that measures the degree of learning by the individual, the behavioural change and the degree of improvement in business effectiveness.
- And finally, a structured approach to measuring the impact of coaching on organisational success should include the

five steps of preparation, design, implementation, analysis and communication of findings.

References

Carter, A. and Peterson, D. P. (2006) Evaluating coaching programmes. In J. Passmore (Ed.) *Excellence in Coaching*. London: Kogan Page.

Chartered Institute of Personnel and Development (2010) *Learning and Talent Development Survey*. London: CIPD. Available at: http://www.cipd.co.uk/hr-resources/survey-reports/default.aspx.

Clutterbuck, D. and Megginson, D. (2005) *Making Coaching Work: Creating a Coaching Culture*. London: CIPD.

Cross, K. F. and Lynch, R. L. (1988) The SMART way to define and sustain success. *National Productivity Review*, 8(1), 23–33.

Kirkpatrick, D. L. (1994, 1996 reprint) *Evaluating Training Programmes: The Four Levels*. San Francisco: Berrett-Koehler.

Leedham, M. (2005) The coaching scorecard: A holistic approach to evaluating the business benefits of coaching. *International Journal of Evidence Based Coaching and Mentoring*, 3(2), 30–44.

Sherman, S. and Freas, A. (2004) The Wild West of executive coaching. *Harvard Business Review*, 82(11), 82–90.

Further reading

Carter, A. (2006) *Practical Methods for Evaluating Coaching*. IES Research Report No. 430. Brighton, UK: Institute for Employment Studies.

12

When to use an external coach and how to ensure the credibility and appropriateness of your external coach

Dawn Forman

The professionalisation of coaching in organisations has developed considerably since first being translated into the workplace in America in the 1970s from its origins in sports coaching. As we have seen, coaching is no longer limited by the coach's expertise in the subject matter, but depends more on their ability to encourage the individual to access their own knowledge and experience to find their own solutions and ways of working that best suit them. This is more effective in providing long-term capability and confidence building than the original concept of the sports coach, where the coach offers solutions to the problem posed.

Table 12.1 provides current definitions of coaching (Jarvis, 2010).

The ability of a coach to know when to be directive or non-directive, as well as the use of coaching techniques, can only develop with experience and practice so, while we encourage all managers to undertake coaching in their workplace, there are times when an experienced external coach may be advantageous.

Coaches can at times be expected to be more directive, as the model in Figure 12.1 (adapted from Heron, 1975) indicates.

Table 12.1 Definitions of coaching

Definition	Author
A process that enables learning and development to occur and thus performance to improve	Parsloe (1999)
Unlocking a person's potential to maximise their own performance	Whitmore (1996)
The overall purpose of coach-mentoring is to provide help and support for people in an increasingly competitive and pressurised world in order to help them: • develop their skills • improve their performance • maximise their potential • become the person they want to be	Jarvis (2004)
Primarily a short-term intervention aimed at performance improvement or developing a particular competence	Clutterbuck (2003)
A conversation, or series of conversations, one person has with another	Starr (2003)
The art of facilitating the performance, learning and development of another	Downey (1999)
Defines the verb 'coach' as: tutor, train, give hints to, prime with facts	Concise Oxford Dictionary
A coach is a collaborative partner who works with the learner to help them achieve goals, solve problems, learn and develop	Caplan (2003)
Meant to be a practical, goal-focused form of personal, one-on-one learning for busy executives and may be used to improve performance or executive behaviour, enhance a career or prevent derailment, and work through organisational issues or change initiatives. Essentially, coaches provide executives with feedback they would normally never get about personal, performance, career and organisational issues	Hall *et al.* (1999)

Table 12.1 Continued

Definition	Author
A collaborative, solution-focused, results-orientated and systematic process in which the coach facilities the enhancement of work performance, life experience, self-directed learning and personal growth of the coachee	Grant (2001)

Adapted from Jarvis (2010).

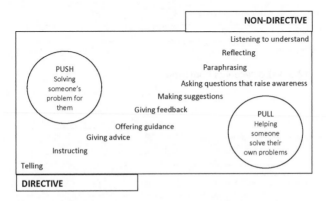

Figure 12.1 Directive–non-directive coaching

Recent research undertaken by the Institute for Leadership and Management (2011) shows the number of institutions using coaching (Figure 12.2), the level of staff receiving coaching in those organisations (Figure 12.3), who undertook the internal coaching (Figure 12.4), the reasons why organisations were using coaching (Figure 12.5) and the methods used to evaluate the success of coaching (Figure 12.6).

Using an external coach

At senior management levels or if a difficult scenario is presented (perhaps an area where an internal coach feels it would be appropriate to refer to someone with more

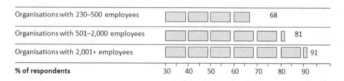

Figure 12.2 **Organisations using coaching**

Figure 12.3 **Who receives coaching**

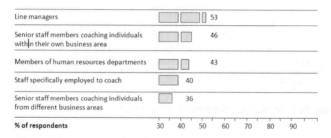

Figure 12.4 **Who undertakes internal coaching**

experience), an external accredited coach may be used. Many professional coaches will have undertaken a programme of study, and an outline of what will be included in such a programme is provided in Figure 12.7.

At senior levels of the organisation the external coach may not only be accredited but will have specialised in executive coaching.

Typical topics that an external executive coach will cover are:

• Greater self-insight through 360-degree feedback, psychometric instruments, coach's feedback.

Individual – for general personal development	53%
Individual – to improve a specific area of performance	26%
Training and development – as part of a wider management or leadership development programme	21%
Individual – to provide development for senior management	19%
Individual – to enable progression within an organisation	12%
Organisation – to support achievement of specific organisational objectives/aims	12%
Individual – to address a specific behavioural issue	8%
Individual – to provide support after a change in position or responsibilities	6%
Individual – to provide support to new employees	5%
Organisation – to support organisational or transformational change	4%
Individual – to engage with or address individual employee concerns	2%
Other	2%
Don't know	1%
Base: All organisations that offer coaching	(196)

Figure 12.5 Why organisations use coaching

Via the existing appraisal system	70%
Measurement against key performance indicators or goals	48%
360 degree appraisal	40%
Specific evaluations for coaching interventions	39%
Employee feedback forms	3%
Informally	3%
Feedback from line managers	1%
Depends on individual or situation	1%
Other	2%
None	6%
Base: All organisations that offer coaching	(196)

Figure 12.6 Methods used to evaluate the success of coaching

- Greater insight into others through discussion and observation.
- Improved relationship management of key stakeholders; more effective influencing and negotiating.

Figure 12.7 **Using an external coach**

- Sharper communication skills; for example, learning more effective ways to run and contribute to meetings.
- More satisfying work–life balance and improved health through more effective time and stress management.
- Releasing potential in team members through more effective:
  - delegation
  - feedback
  - coaching.
- Organisational development: learning to apply systems thinking.
- Career management: identifying next steps; core personal 'brand'; dealing with assessment centres, interviews and other selection processes.

Examples of where the use of an external accredited coach has been effective are usually where there has been a direct impact on the bottom line. Such real examples are given by Meason (cited in Jarvis, 2004):

- Senior partner in an international accounting practice who had failed to win six out of six tenders at the presentation stage. Work with his coach established that he had been relying on a series of unhelpful assumptions and behaviours. He and his coach planned a series of alternative behaviours. These were practised at the session. Result: client won £2.5 million of work for his practice over the next six months.

- Chief executive of a teaching hospital inherited a large deficit on taking over the job and the deficit was still intact at the end of his first year. The Department of Health was exerting considerable pressure to get rapid improvement. Typical behaviour of the chief executive before coaching was to do everything himself, including trying to do the financial director's job; the financial director was on the verge of leaving, feeling demoralised; and the chief executive's marriage was in trouble through his long hours at work. During coaching, the client learnt the difference between delegating and dumping, and also how to manage important relationships more effectively. Result: the deficit halved in the second year and reduced to zero in the third; the chief executive's marriage was greatly improved.

- The director of retail in a large chain was the focus of intense discontent from his team, who resented what they saw as his authoritarian style. The chain was struggling in its highly competitive market. The loss of its talented buying team to competitors would have been intolerable. The director learnt through coaching how to recognise when direction was needed and how to influence more subtly. Within a year the organisation was reporting significantly improved results. The chief executive directly attributed a significant part of this improvement to the changed behaviour – and the coaching – of the director of retail.

When selecting an external coach, it is advisable to consider the points in Table 12.2.

Table 12.2 Selecting an external coach

Area	Possible questions to ask if information has not been gathered from CVs
Previous coaching experience	How long have you worked as a coach? In what kinds of organisations and industry sectors have you worked? At what levels in an organisation have you worked? How many hours of coaching have you delivered? What kinds of issues/problems have you coached individuals on?
References	Are you able to provide us with references from previous clients?
Membership of professional bodies	Are you a member of any professional bodies? If yes, at what level? Do you adhere to a code of ethics/conduct as part of your membership of a professional body?
Qualifications/ training	What training/qualifications have you undertaken relating to your coaching practice? Please describe any development activities you have undertaken in the past year as continuing professional development. Are you qualified to use any psychometric tests?
Relevant experience	Please describe your business experience. What experience/understanding do you have of the [specific organisation/industry] environment?
Professional indemnity insurance	Do you hold professional indemnity insurance? If yes, with whom and to what level?
Supervision	How do you maintain your objectivity and perspective during coaching assignments? What activities do you undertake to keep your skills up to date and ensure you are keeping abreast of professional developments in the field of coaching? Do you think supervision is important for coaching professionals? What formal supervision arrangements do you currently have in place? Do you have your own coach or supervisor? What are their credentials?

Table 12.2 Continued

Area	Possible questions to ask if information has not been gathered from CVs
Establishing the coaching framework/ process	How do you suggest we should evaluate the success/impact of the coaching? Can you describe the theoretical framework you use for the coaching you deliver? What tools/techniques/models do you like to use?

Adapted from Jarvis (2010).

Conclusion

Table 12.3, adapted from Megginson and Boydell (1979), gives a summary of the factors that help or hinder coaching in organisations.

Table 12.3 Factors which help or hinder coaching

Helping factors	Hindering factors
Formal system	
Management by objectives system – gives areas for improvement	Over-identification of coaching with formal assessment system
Appraisal system – with encouragement for self-appraisal	Appraisal system only paid lip-service
Recognition of importance of first few years of manager's career	Lack of evidence that coaching pays off
Money spent on disseminating ideas	
Appraisal system used in deciding promotions	
Other learning opportunities	
Range of functions to move people into – willingness to do so	Internal training courses seen as a chore – unrelated to job
Promotion needs – meaning some movement up the organisation	No follow up of courses attended by managers
Policy of promotion from within	Too frequent movement of managers – can lead subordinates to lose heart

Table 12.3 **Continued**

Helping factors	Hindering factors
Internal training courses seen as development opportunities	
Links with other organisations used	
Using problems faced by the organisation as a basis for discussion by all concerned	
The learner	
Manager and colleagues agree learner's development plan	Lack of commitment to own development
	Sense of powerlessness
The learning climate	
Development of subordinates seen as important	Daily work pressures seen as precluding development activities
Teamwork emphasised	Conflict between groups in organisation
Management style – involves people, gives responsibility, accepts mistakes as learning opportunities	'Top-down' management
	Need for coaching not seen – complacency about performance
	Insecurity – fear of self-examination
Use of an accredited external coach	
Knowing when to use an external accredited coach	Not using selection criteria for the choice of an external accredited coach
Not checking the appropriateness of the accreditation body	

Table 12.3 Continued

Helping factors	Hindering factors
Use of an accredited external executive coach	
Agreeing within the organisation the level and circumstances where an external coach would be appropriate	Not checking the experience of the executive coach and the impact they have made in an organisation similar to yours

Adapted from Megginson and Boydell (1979).

References

Caplan, J. (2003) *Coaching for the Future: How Smart Companies Use Coaching and Mentoring*. London: CIPD.

Clutterbuck, D. (2003) *Creating a Coaching Climate*. London: Clutterbuck Associates.

Downey, M. (1999) *Effective Coaching*. London: Orion Business Books.

Grant, A. M. (2001) *Towards a Psychology of Coaching*. Sydney: Coaching Psychology Institute, School of Psychology, University of Sydney.

Hall, D. T., Otazo, K. L. and Hollenbeck, G. P. (1999) Behind closed doors: What really happens in executive coaching. *Organizational Dynamics*, 28 (perspectives), 39–53.

Heron, J. (1975) *Helping the Client*. London: Sage.

Institute of Leadership and Management (2009) *Creating a Coaching Culture*. London: IPD.

Jarvis, J. (2010) *Coaching and Buying Coaching Services*. London: CIPD.

Megginson, D. and Boydell, T. (1979) *A Manager's Guide to Coaching*. London: BACIE.

Parsloe, E. (1999) *The Manager as Coach and Mentor*. London: Institute of Personnel and Development.

Starr, J. (2003) *The Coaching Manual*. London: Pearson Education.

Whitmore, J. (1996) *Coaching for Performance* (2nd ed.). London: Nicholas Brearley.

Index